William Bagshawe

William Bagshawe was born within a stone's throw of this – the oldest – cottage in Litton, 1639. As a boy of 11 he would no doubt watch it being built

William Bagshawe

The Apostle of the Peak

JOHN M. BRENTNALL

THE BANNER OF TRUTH TRUST

THE BANNER OF TRUTH TRUST
78b Chiltern Street, London WIM IPS
*

© *John M. Brentnall* 1970
First printed 1970
*

Set in 11 *on* 12pt *Monotype Imprint* 101
and printed in Great Britain by
Billing & Sons Limited
Guildford and London

Contents

Illustrations

Preface

The sources of information about Bagshawe are few. In the first place, no appreciation of him can be undertaken without the biography by his nephew, John Ashe, published in 1704. Ashe's careful attention to detail, based on a sympathetic and intimate acquaintance with the great preacher, renders his report invaluable. Every magazine article and biographical note on Bagshawe consists of little more than gleanings from Ashe.

Second in importance is a memoir of the 'Apostle' by one of his descendants. W. H. G. Bagshawe's portrait benefits from his extensive use of unpublished manuscripts which have been preserved in the family since the preacher's death.

I am greatly indebted to Bagshawe's present descendant, Major F. E. G. Bagshawe, who has kindly permitted me to study the 'Apostle's' unpublished treatises, sermon-notes, commentaries and part-diary.

Also I would like to thank the Editorial Department of the Banner of Truth Trust and particularly Mr S. M. Houghton, whose suggestions have been most valuable; Mr Frank Rodgers for his excellent photographs and my wife and Mr John Ward for their reading of the proofs.

Bagshawe's Genealogy

m, 1449
Nicholas Bagshawe of Wormhill & Abney = Alicia, *d,* & co-heir of John Hall of Hucklow

William Bagshawe of Abney = *d,* of Browne of Chapel-en-le-Frith

Nicholas Bagshawe = Eliz, *d,* of Humphrey Ruggeley of Longdon, Staffs

Nicholas Bagshawe = Jane, *d,* of   William   Osmond   Robert   Thomas
of Farewell, Staffs. Robert Lynacre

Edward Bagshawe of Wormhill, = Eliz, *d,* of Robert Greatore
Abney & Hucklow   of Greatorex in Wormhill

Eliz Bagshawe,   Margaret,
d, unmarried   *d,* unmarried 1559

Nicholas Bagshawe = Isabell,   John   Robert   Ralph
          d, of Robert Benbridge of Wormhill

Henry Bagshawe = Ann,   George   Robert   Ann   Elizabeth   Alicia   Margaret
        d, of John Barker
        of Abney

6 Aug. 1625
William Bagshawe = Jane, *d,* of Ralph Oldfield of Litton   Robert
of Wormhill,
Abney & Litton,   = Ellen, *d,* of Robert Bagshawe of Taddington, & 2nd wife
b, 16 Aug. 1598,
d, 1669

16 Jun. 1651
WILLIAM   = Agnes,   John Bagshawe   Susannah, *m,*   Adam Bagshawe
BAGSHAWE   *d,* of Peter Barker   of Litton &   1st William Barber,   of Wormhill
        of Darley,   Great Hucklow   2nd Edward Ashe
        buried 14 Nov.   *d,* 4 Nov. 1703
        1701

20 Apr. 1685
John Bagshawe   Samuel Bagshawe of Ford = Sarah,
b, 8 Jan. 1654   *b,* 31 Dec. 1656   *d,* of Samuel Child
buried 25 May 1664   buried 11 Dec. 1706   of Leeds

x

I

Birth and Early Life (1628-43)

'One of the most devoted and heroic men the 17th century produced' . . . 'He attained such degrees of grace as very few arrive at' . . . 'St. Paul was not a better man than he' . . . 'He is "nobilissimus" in the Bagshawe pedigree.' These are but a few of the praises lavished upon a man who, to friend and foe alike, was the embodiment of Christian ideals in Derbyshire. That the name of William Bagshawe became a household word in cottage and hall for over two hundred years after his death, and that even today it commands respect among Nonconformists of the High Peak of his native county, is ample testimony to the quality of his life and to the contribution he made to historic Christianity.

Born on January 17th, 1628, in Litton Hall, high up on the Peakland plateau overlooking the picturesque Wye valley, William Bagshawe was the eldest son of William and Jane Bagshawe. Two days later he was baptised at Tideswell.

His paternal ancestors were noted for their social influence rather than for their religious connections. The Bagshawes of Abney boasted one of the oldest crests in the county and the oldest bearing the name in all England. From the time of Stephen (1135–54), when his forbears had been prominent landowners in the parish of Chapel-en-le-Frith, the future Puritan preacher could trace his genealogy through the leading tenants of the Champayne area of the Royal Forest of the Peak during the reign of Edward I to a number of prosperous Elizabethan gentry in possession of their own estates. Such a reputable line, though of no merit in the reckonings of God's grace, was by no means insignificant in its bearing on the great preacher's life work.

The conspicuous position of power among the gentry of North Derbyshire with which the Abney Bagshawes were associated had been severely undermined by the close of the 16th century. Its recovery can be traced directly to William's father (1598–1669). That he was gifted with great determination and an enormous capacity for work was in the event providential, for immediately after his father's early death, avaricious relatives stepped in and defrauded him of much of his inheritance. By 1625, the year of his marriage, however, the practical advice of friends had combined with his strong sense of family pride and keen business acumen to consolidate his position on the Litton estates and pave the way for a period of increasing prosperity. In the 1630s, he successfully negotiated for extensive farming property in Abney, acquired a number of moieties in the parishes of Glossop and Chapel-en-le-Frith and gained possession of several lead mines in the district. It was, in fact, largely through the current boom in the lead industry that the foundations of the future wealth of his family were laid. By the time of his death, the elder William Bagshawe had not only restored the depleted resources of the Abney line, he had, by God's rich blessing, gained for it a double measure of its former affluence, leaving his three sons 'all opulent and respected', owners of sizeable properties at Ford, Great Hucklow and Wormhill.

Litton Hall, the ancestral home of the Earl of Litton, was the centre of young William Bagshawe's world for the first fifteen years of his life. From the windows of its spacious and comfortable rooms he would regularly watch his father leave to spend the day on his estates, supervising the work there. The sheep required folding and shearing, the stone-walling surrounding the fields needed his constant attention, skins were to be cured, butter and cheese processed, and a dozen duties called for the master's personal supervision.

It can be imagined that William, who showed a lively interest in the world around him, rarely refused an invitation to accompany his father across the moors to the popular fairs at Chapel-en-le-Frith and Hathersage, where the products of his extensive breeding were sold and exchanged for other livestock. Visits to the Barmote Court at Monyash, which dealt with the intricate disputes of the lead-mining industry, also engaged his inquisitive mind and filled out his youthful hours. More frequently, he was given the opportunity of a trip to the family lead mines around Litton and Bradwell. Here, where the countryside was heavily scarred by opencast workings, drainage tunnels and shafts, he would see the ore being loaded on to sturdy pack-horses ready for transportation down the valley-side to the smelting furnaces below.

On such journeys, William inevitably became aware of the responsibilities which perhaps one day would be transferred to his own shoulders. He also imbibed something of his father's attitude to life. Pointing out the various country scenes on the way— Monsal Dale, Mam Tor, Edale and the waste plateau of Kinderscout beyond—the elder William Bagshawe often spoke of God's particular goodness in granting him such a 'fair inheritance'. On meeting poor widows and their children during the course of his rounds, he would invariably hand them money, at the same time recalling to his son how God had been to him a Father of the fatherless. His own charity, he acknowledged, was but a token of his debt to God. This atmosphere of gratitude to God and benevolence to others which surrounded William throughout his formative years contributed much towards the moulding of his character and played an important part in his relationships with the local inhabitants of the Peak.

The stability which a happy relationship with his father imparted to William's life was disturbed on only one recorded occasion—when his father was committed to prison. The cause of his imprisonment can be traced to the 'Personal Rule' of Charles I. In order to reconstruct the Royal Navy, which James I had allowed to decay, the King levied a special tax on all his subjects. The parish of Tideswell, to which the inhabitants of Litton belonged, was charged with supplying revenue to build and maintain 'one ship of 350 tons, manned with 140 men, and double equipage, with munition, wages, and victuals'. That the levying of this 'ship-money' caused widespread resentment was to be expected. Of special interest is that William Bagshawe was prepared to organise resistance to the King's demands. Evidently he urged the miners in his employ to present a united opposition to the tax. The result was a threatened riot. 'On August 6th, 1634,' reads a report of the incident, 'a tumultuous assembly of miners was held at Litton, the said miners having intended to present a petition to the King.' As the 'inciter to rebellion', Bagshawe was apprehended and removed to Derby. From the county gaol he wrote a letter to the constable of Tideswell explaining the situation, 'which letter was openly read upon Sunday last after Evening Prayer at the Cross in Tideswell and thereupon the miners came forward upon Monday towards Nottingham', doubtless to beg their master's release and apologise for the disturbance. For how long he remained in prison we have no record, but by his firm stand for what he believed to be the rights of his men, William Bagshawe senior gained for himself and his family a degree of esteem among the High Peak mining communities which many years failed to dissolve.

When young William first experienced the irresistible stirrings of the Holy Spirit in his heart it is impossible to say. John Ashe, his first biographer, relates no more than that he 'had the privilege of an early conversion to God'. For this experience he may have been indebted to the instrumentality of his mother, but we can only surmise. An Oldfield and a devout woman (she was an aunt of the famous John Oldfield, the ejected rector of Carsington), she had made herself responsible for her son's religious training from the first. While her husband was out supervising work on the estates and in the mines, Jane Bagshawe spent many hours with William at her knee, instructing him in Bible knowledge, praying with him, and seeking to encourage any beginnings of spiritual life she could discern in him. We might infer that he knew little of 'the long, dark night of the soul' which preceded many Puritan conversions and that he quickly attained a state of peace with God, for his spiritual struggles never assumed proportions large enough to merit recording.

From the time of his conversion, William began to reveal a keen appetite for spiritual food. Providentially, he sought Christian fellowship and solid instruction where it was to be found. In the elder John Rowlandson, vicar of Bakewell, and Immanuel Bourne of Eastwood Hall, rector of Ashover, he discovered two distinguished men of God whose counsel on difficult passages of Scripture, and on the personal problems he encountered at the outset of his Christian life, earned from their young disciple an almost filial regard.

Rowlandson was revered by Christians throughout the Peak for his unstinting labours for the Gospel and for unity in the things of Christ. A number of praying and Bible-reading families in Bakewell and the surrounding district owed their earliest spiritual awakenings to his instrumentality. The gravity of his demeanour was a byword amongst his parishioners and his fame as a catechist was widespread. At Sheldon and Over Haddon, humble labourers and artisans would carefully prepare their cottages for him, gathering round his feet as he expounded the Word of God to their hearts and questioned them on its eternal truths. The convicting effects of his sermons, coupled with the whole-hearted consecration of his life to God, drew from Bagshawe the observation that he 'not only spoke but lived great things'. To saddle one of his father's horses and ride the three miles into Bakewell was one of the young Puritan's chief delights during these early years of his Christian life.

Immanuel Bourne commanded no less veneration from his zealous young pupil. A staunch Presbyterian who later lost his living for his convictions and gained a reputation as a preacher at Paul's Cross and St. Sepulchre's in the City, Bourne combined in his person the qualities of an educated gentleman and a gracious Christian pastor. As minister of the Gospel at Ashover and squire of Eastwood Hall, he was able to strike up a happy relationship with the Bagshawes on both counts. Friendly family visits became occasions of spiritual fellowship as well as social intercourse. Bourne and his young admirer doubtless spent many hours together poring over such theological treasures as Calvin's commentaries or Luther's *Bondage of the Will* which the older man purposely slipped into his saddle-bag before each journey. Some evidence hints that William regarded Bourne as his spiritual father. Be that as it may, the good old rector's influence on his pupil was considerable.

Bagshawe's encounter with these experienced men of God proved decisive in the shaping of his theological thinking and in the richness of his religious experience. Under their guidance, he soon came to accept the teachings of the Protestant Reformation—God as sovereign of the universe and absolute master of the hearts of men; man as a dependent creature, made in God's image but corrupted through his fall into sin; Jesus Christ as the Mediator of the Covenant of Grace; the Holy Spirit as the indwelling agent of this covenant, uniting believers to God in Christ and sanctifying them; the necessity of regeneration and holiness; the ultimate security of God's people and the certainty of their future destiny as partakers of Christ's glory—these were the great biblical truths which came to be deeply imprinted on Bagshawe's mind.

But not only was his mind enlightened by the beams that shone from the Word of God. He became the humble possessor of a religion which sanctifies the heart. The change which overtook Bagshawe's whole outlook at this period betokens an experimental acquaintance with God. Rowlandson and Bourne must have been quite emphatic in their insistence that God could only be known savingly when men yield themselves entirely to Him, submit to His absolute authority, and regulate every detail of their lives by His precepts, for from the time of their influence, Bagshawe began to devote all his energies to seeking 'to walk holily before God'.

The development of a rich spiritual life did not deny the young student a practical interest in national affairs. On the contrary, the religious and political crisis which overhung the country during the late 1630s and early 1640s caused him, along with the nation as a whole, to turn vigilant eyes to the developments which so seriously threatened the purity and vitality of the Church in England. The uniformitarian policies of Archbishop Laud had by 1638 wrought spiritual havoc among many churches in the southern and eastern counties. By the time of their enforcement on the remote Peakland congregations, deep resentment at his 'Popish innovations' had sprung up, and pockets of resistance had already been forced into Nonconformity. Many who remained within the Anglican fold recognised that Laud's vigorous insistence on worshipping towards an altar, using candles, crucifixes, tapers and copes in the administration of the bread and wine, and bowing at the mention of the Saviour's name, would spell death to evangelical religion unless opposed. Wherever ritualistic observances, they said, such as penance and crossings and genuflexions, replace lively faith, repentance and loving obedience, knowledge of the grace of God is bound to become relegated to the background and the people will perish for lack of vision.

The situation grew more disquieting when the scattered congregations of the Peak heard of severe penal measures against dissenting resistance. In the capital, Calvinistic preachers received whippings; some had their ears cut off and their noses slit; others were committed to the pillory and prison; in addition to which most were heavily fined. Their supporters were likewise fined or imprisoned.

This terrible religious intimidation struck fear for the truth into many Christian hearts, and before 1640 some twenty thousand left the country, facing the hazards of an Atlantic crossing and of pioneer life in the New England and Virginian colonies, where, they believed, the Gospel would be granted a free course.

The remoteness of Derbyshire from the capital, and the inhospitable nature of her terrain, somewhat hindered the application of

Laud's policies. Yet an increasing number of families were being forced out of the local churches, and the trickle of fines and physical punishments which characterise the records of the early 1630s shortly assumed the proportions of a steady stream.

Although he never joined their ranks at this critical time, Bagshawe must have felt keenly the plight of persecuted Nonconformists. His sympathies lay as yet, however, with those who were seeking to reform the Church from within, and to these he turned for instruction and fellowship. Among men of this kind, few proved more valuable to his growth in grace than Anthony Mellor, Robert Craven and Thomas Stanley. Mellor, curate of Sheldon and later Taddington, received the highest praise from the young student. 'Though I did not partake of the fruit thereof (i.e. of his ministerial labours) often, I am well satisfied they were sound and sweet,' he later wrote. 'In all my acquaintance with him,' he added, 'I observed him to be one that was in earnest for the life and power of godliness.' Bagshawe's assessment of Craven, curate at Longstone chapel, was equally favourable. Under his ministry, he claimed, 'I have more than once sitten with delight, and he hath left behind him the memory of one that for his time made good improvement.' Stanley, vicar of Ashford-in-the-Water from 1636 to 1644, probably exercised the most permanent influence of the three. To him more than any other single person can be attributed the seeds of disaffection to the episcopal system which were sown in Bagshawe's mind at this time.

Between his visits to Bakewell, Sheldon, Longstone and Ashford, Bagshawe continued to seek fellowship with the church of his own parish of Tideswell. The incumbents of the living, who came and went with alarming frequency during this period, evidently impressed him little, but one particular occasion supplies an abiding memory. While still 'in childhood', Bagshawe later recalled, 'worthy Mr. Cresswell', chaplain at Lime Hall, Disley, ascended the pulpit one Lord's Day and preached with such overwhelming power and penetration on the text 'There is no peace, saith my God, to the wicked', that an indelible impression of the awe-fulness of God's justice remained on his mind to the end of his life!

Meanwhile, William was receiving his basic formal education, but where, and for how long, remains unknown. Ashe relates no more than that he was sent to 'several country schools'. We can

B

only conjecture that he passed through the traditional channels of learning which led eventually to the curriculum of one of the universities. Theology, with its accessories Hebrew, Greek and Latin; catechetical learning and Scripture memorising; letter-writing; producing and declaiming original orations—these were the disciplines which consumed his energies at school. Over half a century later, Bagshawe recalled that he 'made greater proficiency' at his academic work 'than most of his equals', thereby proving the qualities which were to emerge with such force in his ministry, his great capacity for work, considerable powers of concentration and tenacious memory.

By his fifteenth birthday there was no doubt in William's mind as to the vocation he should pursue. He was determined to enter the Christian ministry. This decision at a major turning-point in his life became the cause of considerable family trouble. His father was resolutely opposed to the idea and did almost everything within his power to dissuade William from it. To succeed as a God-fearing and upright country squire, he believed, would more accord with his son's breeding and talents than to enter the lists against the world, the flesh and the devil. Unless practised in the city or some fashionable resort, he may have argued, the calling of minister held out few hopes of promotion and recognition. What more did William require than to follow in his father's footsteps? The foundations for his success as a landowner had already been firmly laid. Besides, all his achievements in the lead-mining industry would be thrown to the winds were his son to become a parson.

Such considerations, however, did not weigh with the determined young Puritan, so insuperable was his conviction of the divine call. Even the threat of disinheritance, reserved as a final blow with which to shatter his hopes, could not sway his judgement. Completely ignoring the pleas of his family to enter a more lucrative profession, he took steps to prepare for his life's work, and arrangements were made for him to enter the higher sphere of university life.

2

Cambridge (1643-46)

In 1643, William Bagshawe entered Corpus Christi College, Cambridge. His arrival at the university coincided with the beginning of one of the most turbulent periods in the history of the town. Civil war had recently broken out, and under the influence of Oliver Cromwell, the town's M.P. since 1640, Cambridge had become a stronghold for the Parliamentary forces. 'Our town and castle are now very strongly fortified,' Parliament was informed, 'being encompassed by breastworks and bulwarks.' A number of buildings within the town were taken over as barracks, and soldiers were billeted on the townspeople. The comings and goings of troops, the meetings of the various committees of the Eastern Counties Association which sat at the Bear Inn, the burials of plague-smitten townspeople and the destruction of 'Monuments of Superstition and Idolatry' in the various church buildings and college chapels, by order of Parliament, were some of the events Bagshawe witnessed during his stay at the university. Apparently no shots were fired in town while he was there, and the only fear of invasion from the King was a slight one, when, after Naseby, his horses arrived within two miles of the town, only to withdraw to Oxford when challenged by Parliamentary forces. Although evidence on the subject is conflicting, the general opinion of historians of the period is that during Parliamentary occupation of the town the university was little disturbed and students were able to continue their studies in relative peace.

The routine of the day would have appealed to Bagshawe's natural inclinations. He would rise at 5 a.m. in summer and 6 a.m. in winter at the sound of the college bell. After breakfast, the morning would be occupied with lectures and private study. Further study during the afternoon would doubtless be punctuated by walks in and around Cambridge with his college companions. Supper at 5 p.m. was followed by a further period of study and discussion.

Throughout his stay at Corpus Christi, Bagshawe shared a communal room with five or six other students under the care of a Mr. Boise. Described by his pupil as 'a learned but not very active man', Boise was responsible for his students' financial and social arrangements, and prepared them in their first year for the more advanced work to follow.

Bagshawe's gentle breeding, keen intellect and warm disposition no doubt found him many friends at Corpus Christi, but no friendship was allowed to interrupt his programme of work. 'The company of friends, even Christian friends,' he said, 'can become a snare, by shutting out or shortening some duties.' Like Joseph Alleine at Oxford, he accounted time the most precious commodity. 'Be we true mourners,' he would exhort his companions, 'that golden hours, much more precious than gold or pearls, have not been duly improved.' His own private hours were characterised by the most careful study. Marking off with his pencil and committing to memory some of the best learning of the past and of his own day, he gradually made his mind a valuable store-house of biblical, Protestant and Patristic quotations, from which he was later to draw extensively for pulpit and press.

We may be certain that Bagshawe's mature spiritual and intellectual outlook was formed during his three years at Cambridge. His experiences among the North Derbyshire churches had provided the incentive to discover at the deepest level what God has actually spoken to man, how His Word is to be received, understood and interpreted, and in what ways that Word can be most effectively taught. At Cambridge, the opportunity to knit together satisfying answers to such questions into one unified system of religion presented itself.

Bagshawe's inquisitive mind was given plenty of scope in which to exercise itself in these fundamental questions of theology. In the first place his dons were men of the highest standing in the Presbyterian Church of England. The learned Dr. John Arrowsmith, a member of the Westminster Assembly of Divines who accepted the Regius Professorship of Divinity in 1644, was held in awed esteem by the young student. It was he whose lectures and sermons Bagshawe gratefully recalled some fifty years later in an unpublished and untitled manuscript of 1697, and to whose insistence on catechising as an effectual teaching method he expressed great indebtedness. There can be little doubt that

Bagshawe and his fellow students received skeleton outlines of the Westminster Catechisms during Arrowsmith's lectures. It is also likely that from his lips came the most recent news of the Assembly's deliberations and reforms, interwoven with the more formal aspects of his lectures. What is certain is that, under his supervision, Bagshawe was given as solid a grounding in the truths of the Reformed Faith as Cambridge could offer during the mid-17th century. The benefits of tutelage from a man of Arrowsmith's calibre must have been of incalculable value to the young Puritan.

The young Cambridge student was also influenced by Dr. Benjamin Whichcote, who had recently been brought out of the comparative seclusion of a country living to become Provost of King's. Unhappily, Whichcote's orthodoxy was marred by a latitudinarianism which was to have devastating effects on the Church in the following century. The seeds of this teaching were already being sown in the tutorials and sermons which Bagshawe attended in the 1640s. Briefly, it may be summarised as follows: despite the Fall, man still possesses a certain amount of spiritual light (the candle of the Lord, he called it), whereby he may know God and His will as He is revealed in Scripture. He is therefore able to attain Divine Truth solely by the right exercise of his reason.

The fatal factor in this idea is Whichcote's failure to consider that since the Fall, the 'carnal mind' of man is at 'enmity' with God and wholly incapable of perceiving spiritual truth. In seeking reasonable explanations for the supernatural truths of Scripture which transcend reason, Whichcote became guilty of accommodating these truths to the unbelieving mind, thereby leaving his pupils with the impression that only what can be explained is worthy of belief, whereas in fact the Word of God is to be received on trust, independent of our grasp of its contents. Furthermore, if man by nature is able to understand and interpret aright God's Word, he no longer stands in need of the regenerating grace and special illumination of the Holy Spirit. Man has become partly able to save himself.

Whether or not Bagshawe at Cambridge discerned the heretical tendencies underlying Whichcote's thought is not certain, but his later writings are replete with confutations of latitudinarianism.

Meanwhile, alongside his study of Calvin, Perkins and Beza, to whom Whichcote claimed in the 1650s to have devoted most of his lecture time, Bagshawe was sent by his controversial mentor to Plato, Cicero and Plotin. Perhaps he would have agreed with Richard Baxter that Whichcote's evident knowledge and love of the God of the Scriptures were sadly counteracted by a 'mixture of Platonisme, Origenisme, and Arianisme'. At any rate, he always retained a strong aversion to Whichcote's distinguishing ideas, but made frequent use of his orthodox lecture notes.

Of his third don, Dr. Thomas Hill, Master of Trinity and 'a light in the church of God', we hear little more from Bagshawe than that he occasionally preached the university sermon. It is probable, however, that Hill was held in as much esteem as Arrowsmith and Whichcote, no doubt on account of his famed concern for the welfare of his students, as well as his formidable learning and Christian piety.

In addition to the personal influence of his dons, Bagshawe, through the medium of literature, came into contact with some of the choicest spirits and finest minds of Protestantism. The incisive brilliance and superb exegesis of Calvin, the heart-stirring sermons of Richard Sibbes, and the weighty, provocative treatises of Thomas Cartwright, William Perkins and John Preston, to name no others, exercised a profound influence on his receptive mind. Through their instrumentality he became thoroughly grounded in the religion which Dr. Warfield has described as 'Christianity come into its own'. Certainly, at Cambridge Bagshawe became an intelligent and tenacious adherent of Calvinism. From it he was never to turn for the remaining fifty-six years of his life.

In 1646 Bagshawe graduated B.A. from Corpus Christi and returned to his native county. That he pursued no postgraduate course is to be seen in the light of his strong inclination to begin his ministerial probationship without delay.

3

Preparation for the Ministry
(1646-50)

By the close of 1646, Bagshawe's home had witnessed a number of important changes. His brother John, at eleven years of age, had already become prospective heir to the family estates. A sister Susannah, of whom William was very fond, was in her teens when he came down from Cambridge, and in November, 1646, a further brother, Adam, was added to the family. From this time we hear nothing more of Bagshawe's mother; possibly she died in child-birth or shortly afterwards. Sometime after her death William's father married again, taking for his wife Ellen, the daughter of Robert Bagshawe of Taddington.

For the eighteen months between his graduation and the commencement of his probationship, Bagshawe continued his studies in Litton Hall, resorting frequently to the mature spiritual counsel and theological teaching of John Rowlandson and Immanuel Bourne. Bearing this in mind, Bagshawe's later judgement, that he entered 'too rashly on the awful work' of the ministry, is to be received with caution. Ashe's more objective testimony states that Bagshawe was unwilling to take on himself the pastoral care of others without first satisfying himself with 'many thoughts of heart about his own soul and its everlasting concernments', while Bagshawe himself was never in doubt about the genuineness of his call. The depths to which his feelings of inadequacy may have sunk must not blind us to the fact that few men have given such solid proof of their calling as he. The entire fifty-four years of his ministerial life were so richly blessed by God that we must attribute his statement to an underestimation of the grace given to him.

His first ventures in public reading and preaching of the Word of God were confined to the village of Wormhill. Here, in the quaintly-towered 13th-century chapel of St. Margaret, surrounded by yews and overlooking stately Wormhill Hall, Bagshawe spent the opening months of 1648 as a probationer. It is certain from the consequences that he did not depend upon his own feeble resources in his preaching, but that he trusted in God for the Word to be proclaimed 'not with enticing words of man's wisdom, but in demonstration of the Spirit and of power'. The singular authority and acceptance which accompanied his addresses had important repercussions immediately, for barely three months of the year had elapsed when he was called to exercise his ministry in a much wider sphere. On the eve of his twenty-first birthday he was invited to become an assistant presbyter in Sheffield. Under the supervision of James Fisher, the incumbent of St. Peter's, he was allotted responsibility for the care of the church at Attercliffe.

At the time of Bagshawe's arrival there, Attercliffe was an attractive country village. Land which is today covered by rows of terraced houses and grimy factories was then graced by an open common and a loosely-knit group of cottages whose occupants were employed by the two prominent families of the district, the Brights of Carbrook Hall and the Spencers of Attercliffe Hall. The small chapel, erected by local Christians in 1629, secured attention by its relatively isolated position on the common boundary. Situated two miles from the parish church in Sheffield, it was recommended by the Parliamentary commissioners of 1649 for parish status at the earliest convenience.

The people to whom Bagshawe now ministered had already received a firm grounding in the Reformed Faith under their first pastor, Stanley Gower, an eminent Westminster divine and sponsor of John Owen's *Death of Death*, and his successor, James Bright. Now, six years after reorganisation along Presbyterian lines, the church was without its own pastor, having been dependent for its ministry since 1642 on visiting elders from the local presbytery. Bagshawe was therefore given full pastoral charge of the church.

The moving spirit behind the building of the chapel at Attercliffe had been Colonel John Bright. He had made handsome donations to the work, 'beautified the quier with sentences of Scripture at his own charge', acquired stone and timber for the building, procured a bell and donated a Bible. Each Lord's Day, morning and afternoon, he and his wife, accompanied by their older children, filed into the family pew, followed by the servants and tenantry. As their new minister, Bagshawe ascended the pulpit and proceeded to dispense to them the words of life. 'Hath the free grace of God the Father in Jesus Christ been much the matter of thine admiration?' he enquired of them. 'O may free grace fill all your hearts! May it run and be glorified in all your houses. May your beds, boards, shops, fields, savour of your profiting by the doctrine of it. . . . The word of grace does not reach all people or places, and the powerful dispensing of it does not reach all. There are many nations that have never heard whether there be a Christ or no; and there is a speciality in grace as to the inward effects of it. . . . There was great storming at this doctrine when our Saviour had taught that there were many widows, and the prophet only sent to her of Sarepta. . . . I have long been affected by a speech of famous Luther, that though ministers are much opening the mystery of the Gospel and the grace of God, yet many of their hearers, when their turn cometh that they must die, see too too little into it. May it not be so of you!'

Colonel Bright and his family overlooked the angularity of the novice's earliest addresses in their admiration of his fervent spirit and plain dealing with their souls. One who spoke so faithfully to those of high degree, they prophesied, would before long make his mark upon the peasantry and tradesmen of the district.

After service, Bagshawe returned to Carbrook Hall with Colonel Bright, who had invited him on his arrival in Attercliffe to undertake the duties of domestic chaplain to his family, offering him rooms in his home. Leading the household in family worship each morning and evening, catechising the children and servants, and advising members of the family on spiritual matters, were the duties his appointment entailed. In addition to such formal duties, occasions were not wanting for the zealous young chaplain to hold forth the torch of truth which God had entrusted to him, for John Bright, generous and public-spirited, kept open table at Carbrook. Members of the local gentry, ministers of the Gospel, officers engaged in the civil wars, and students, all found a welcome at his home. The following discussion, drawn from Bagshawe's writings, may give us some idea of the informal conversation which graced Bright's hospitable table:

Present: Col. John Bright and his wife, William Spencer of Attercliffe Hall, James Fisher of St. Peter's, the local schoolmaster and Bagshawe.

Bright: Is there such an evidence and appearance of a national returning to God as our endeavours called for during the late wars?

Fisher: Blessed be the Lord, there is blood truly royal running in the veins of some of England's grandees. What say you, William?

Bagshawe: O that we could prove this concerning all who wear coronets! If there are those who appear zealous for a particular form, O that there were evidences they were zealous for the power of godliness!

Mrs. Bright: There are ministers, both of one denomination and another, who magnify their office.

Schoolmaster: Aye, and judges too. England has great cause to bless God that she has lawyers and judges of the disposition of Mr. Hale.

Spencer: But are all worthy of such a commendation? Are not too many too willing to breed suits, and too willing to protract them?

Fisher: And are there not too many whose eloquence is used to maintain unjust causes?

Bright: But if we come a little nearer home, we must surely notice that we ourselves (glancing at Spencer) have husbandmen, and I look on the husbandman's calling to be as honourable as any, who take God with them whenever they go into the fields.

Bagshawe: And miners, too! Through the rich grace of God, there are miners who not only dig into the bowels of the earth, but into the bowels of the Scripture: but alas, go to the generality of those who labour in the mines, and you will find that they are not such labourers as we would commend.

Bright: We profess highly, but what fruits, what summer fruits do we gather and bear in this summer season? It is a summer time as to Gospel privileges. Is it so as to our bearing Gospel fruits?

It was on such occasions as this, as well as in the discharging of his chaplaincy duties, that Bagshawe's patrons became so impressed with his spirituality. The affection and zeal with which he undertook the instruction of their children and servants, combined with his particular seriousness in preaching and visiting, were so evidently in advance of his years that on Bright's recommendation the local presbytery pressed for his ordination a year before he reached the stipulated age of twenty-four.

4

Ordination and Marriage (1651)

For a clear understanding of the events surrounding Bagshawe's ordination, some explanation of the rise of Presbyterianism is required. The resistance of the Scots to the attempt of Charles I and Archbishop Laud to impose prelacy on Scotland, where the Presbyterian system of Calvin had taken firm hold, had evoked strong sympathy in England. This was reflected in the Long Parliament (1641–60), the last to be called by Charles. When the Commons divided into Royalists and Parliamentarians (Cavaliers and Roundheads), a goodly proportion of the latter held Presbyterian convictions. In December, 1641, the Commons presented to the King their Grand Remonstrance in which they asked for a General Synod of Divines to be called to consider the reformation of religion. Some, indeed, hoped for a drawing together of England and Scotland. The ultimate outcome was the Westminster Assembly and Confession of Faith.

Before the Assembly was well under way a second cause of Presbyterian pressure had emerged. The New Model Army had not yet appeared on the scene, and Parliament, in taking up arms against King Charles, appealed to Scotland for military aid. 'The shrewd northern mind saw the chance of a godly bargain,' explains the late E. J. Poole-Connor. 'The help asked was promised on one condition: that the English leaders should adopt the Scottish Covenant—their great witness to the faith of Calvin and Knox. This they consented to do.' On September 22nd, 1643, when the House of Commons and the Westminster Assembly of Divines gathered in St. Margaret's, Westminster, to take the Solemn League and Covenant, Presbyterianism became the official religion of the nation. Parliament consented to accept it and impose it in place of episcopacy.

When the First Civil War ended, however, the New Model Army, swayed by Independents, fell apart from Parliament, controlled as it was by Presbyterians, and pursued its own course. A Second Civil War followed which terminated with the victory of the New Model Army, the execution of the King, and, after an interval, the setting up of the Commonwealth. Meanwhile committees were operating to ensure that none but godly men, preferably of Puritan bent, were appointed to vacant livings.

Despite the dearth of ministers after the Laudian persecutions—for some had been driven abroad and the ravages of civil war had killed others—the requirements for admission to the Christian ministry were commendably stringent during the 'Westminster' and Cromwellian periods. No counsels of expediency would compel the Westminster divines to lower their standards in order to fill vacant pulpits. In Derbyshire, where Presbyterianism was applied more consistently and for a longer period apparently than in many other counties, these requirements were scrupulously observed. Several candidates of questionable orthodoxy, defective learning, lax morality or inadequate pastoral ability were refused ordination.

Before he could qualify for the work of the ministry, testimonials respecting Bagshawe's subscription to the Covenant of the Three Kingdoms, his university degree and his godliness required the approval of the local presbytery. Rowlandson and Bourne, both of whom sat on the presbytery for the Hundred of Scarsdale, which examined Bagshawe, probably vouchsafed for him on these counts. He was then interviewed for proof of 'the grace of God in him' and his learning, and for evidence of his vocation to the ministry. This interview was apparently held on the last day of 1650. We can readily surmise the scene and the proceedings.

Members of the presbytery, among whom were James Hewit (Baslow), John Billingsley (Chesterfield), Robert Moore (Brampton), Richard Maudsley (Dronfield), and John Rowlandson (Bakewell), under the moderatorship of Immanuel Bourne (Ashover), faced the candidate across a long oak table. The presbytery's clerk recorded the proceedings at a small desk in the corner of the room. After prayer, the interrogation:

Bourne: Tell me, my son, what is a sign of true grace?
Bagshawe: When there is most of patience as to injuries offered to ourselves and least of forbearance as to what strikes at God.
(An auspicious opening!)
Bourne: We hear you are shortly to be married. When you have

taken a wife and received a call to a church, you will be head of your own house. What do heads of houses need to be?

Bagshawe: Prudent heads, who understand how to apply themselves suitably to those under them; watchful, lest the cord of their authority be loosed; believing—when they plant and water, waiting through Christ's merit for the increase.

(The questioning now passes to Hewit.)

Hewit: What do you count the lust of the flesh, the lust of the eyes, and the pride of life, spoken of in 1 John 2 : 16?

Bagshawe: The lust of the flesh, that is voluptuousness, self-pleasing; the lust of the eyes, that is covetousness, self-profiting; the pride of life, that is self-exalting. Are not these accounted the world's trinity, as the carnal mind is these in unity?

(Maudsley next takes his turn.)

Maudsley: Give your reply to the Laudian prelates whose excuse for bowing their knees at the name of Jesus is that celebrated text, Philippians 2 : 10.

Bagshawe: I doubt not the word 'name' is in this text, as in divers others, to be construed not for the bare syllables thereof, for the mere word is not the object of faith or adoration; but, of Christ's name, we are to understand His person, as clothed with His power and authority. I doubt not, by bowing at or in His name is meant subjection to Him and worship of Him.

(Rowlandson now pursues the inquiry.)

Rowlandson: Seeing that God is good, is all good, yea, is goodness itself, and seeing that goodness is the great attractive of love, how can it be that any men or women should hate Him?

Bagshawe: That there is such a sin in the world as hating of God cannot be doubted by those who are past doubting as to the truth and divine authority of the Scriptures. A whole company of men are branded with this crime, Romans 1 : 30, where it is said of all the heathen that they are haters of God. Though none do hate God under the notion of goodness, yet persons do hate God as He is the Father and Fountain of holiness—as He sets forth a righteous law which crosses their lusts, and as He will take vengeance on those who obey not that law.

(Perceiving the candidate's fine grasp of these points, Bourne intimates to Bagshawe that he must now read and translate into Latin selected passages from the Hebrew and Greek Testaments. This part of the examination being performed, the test proceeds through logic, philosophy and other branches of learning. After further trying Bagshawe's knowledge of biblical chronology, church history and theological writings generally, Bourne and his colleagues decide to prove the young candidate's skill in defending orthodox doctrine against heresy. Maudsley takes upon himself the role of adversary and introduces the Socinian question.)

Maudsley: Would you deny that reason is man's excellency, and is of great advantage to a Christian?

Bagshawe: Reason is man's excellency, but the Socinians advance and cry it up unreasonably, and under the colour of it do reject plain revelation, and will not believe further than the light within them can see a reason for what is revealed, and who bring down God, and His Word, to be tried at their bar.

(This spirited reply pleases the examiners. The test continues):

Maudsley: Why do you assert special illumination to be necessary to a saving knowledge of Scripture, when reason is the instrument of God for conveying light to the soul?

Bagshawe: They detract from Scripture, when they who may use their reason as an instrument, will set it up as a judge, whether such and such a text, and truth, though plainly delivered, is to be received.

Maudsley: Can you prove that the Socinians deny the Lord that bought them?

Bagshawe: They deny the deity of the Lord Jesus Christ. With them He is not God by nature, only by office. They detract from the value and sufficiency of the price laid down for sin, for they do not hold Christ's sufferings to be propitiatory and satisfactory.

Maudsley: You say they detract from the Godhead; but do they not profess a supreme, sovereign Being?

Bagshawe: Though they will not deny that there is a supreme, sovereign Being, of His being Three in One they will not hear; nor do they fully believe His omnipresence and omniscience. Are not His attributes in their books only qualities? And do they not represent the Lord Christ only as a divine man, and the Holy Ghost as only the virtue of God?

(Having elicited from the candidate the answers they require, these painstaking stewards of God remind Bagshawe of the subject on which he is to preach that evening, and proceed to the final item on this delicate subject.)

Rowlandson: Should Christians play at cards and dice, and encourage their children so to do?

Bagshawe: Some choice men are on this question very sharp. One calls dice 'the Devil's bones' and the cards his 'books'. It is said that all the French Protestants and Dutch divines condemn such plays as lotteries, in which there is a special appeal to Divine Providence, not to be used save in serious matters; also as attended with very evil effects and dispositions. They who plead for some lawful use of them require so many cautions in the users as are next to impossible to be observed. Without doubt, the unregenerate have something else to do than gaming. And as for the regenerate, though some of them may have use for recreations, yet they should be used rarely and inoffensively. If cards be lawful, they are not convenient.

(At this point Bagshawe's examiners decide to terminate the first part of his test. Before leaving the room, Bagshawe deposits his Latin thesis and Confession of Faith in the hands of the clerk, doubtless encouraged by the favourable reception the presbyters have given him.)

January 1st, 1651, was a momentous day for the young candidate. During the morning he was informed that his address, entitled 'Christ's Purchase', delivered before the presbytery the previous evening, had been well received and that his thesis had been 'perused and approved'. The service of ordination would take place that afternoon.

When the appointed time arrived, an unusually large congregation, drawn from the local churches of Scarsdale and the High Peak, settled itself in the old parish church building at Chesterfield, having prepared for the anticipated occasion by prayer and fasting, beseeching God to fill the ordinand with the Spirit of Christ. Bourne preached on the office and duties of a Christian minister. Billingsley, whose church was host for the day, proceeded after the sermon to catechise Bagshawe 'concerning his faith in Christ Jesus, and his persuasion of the truth of the Reformed religion, according to the Scriptures', to inquire into his diligence concerning prayer, reading, meditation, preaching, administering the sacraments, church discipline and other pastoral duties, to seek proof of his zeal for the Gospel and the unity of the Church, and finally to gain assurance of his 'care that himself and his family' would be 'unblameable, and examples to the flock'. When each member of the presbytery had registered his approval of Bagshawe's replies, they in turn solemnly set him apart to the office of the ministry by the laying on of hands, while Immanuel Bourne offered a 'short prayer or blessing'. A brief word of exhortation from Bourne, first to Bagshawe, then to the whole congregation, was followed by the singing of a metrical psalm, after which the assembly was dismissed with a blessing.

For a further six months after his ordination Bagshawe remained in the charge at Attercliffe. During this period he received a call to fill the vacant living of Glossop, in the High Peak, the acceptance of which was to have highly significant consequences in the spiritual history of the county.

Meanwhile, the circumstances of his probationship had brought Bagshawe into contact with the family of Peter Barker, of Darley, whose daughter Agnes he now sought in marriage. The Barkers appear to have been of yeoman stock and decidedly Puritan convictions, being one of the families in the district who had attended the 'illegal' ministrations of the zealous Charles Broxholm, before his death in 1647 a courageous leader of dissent in the Peak. ' 'Tis my joy,' wrote Bagshawe, 'that in the family out of which I had my dear wife (tho' in too few others), he was encouraged.' Whole-heartedly subscribing to the Westminster standard that 'such as marry are to marry in the Lord', Bagshawe first ensured that the bride he sought was a woman after his own heart. Then, having proved her qualities in other spheres, he secured the permission of her father, and on June 11th, 1651, he and Agnes Barker became husband and wife.

5

Glossop (1651-62)

Bagshawe accepted the living of Glossop about six months after his ordination. That he did not supplant an extruded vicar is certain from the report of the Parliamentary Commissioners a year earlier, that there was 'no minister for the present'. The parish register records in Bagshawe's own hand that he was 'called to and employed in ye cure of soules in Glossope ye 24 of June, 1651'. Here, in the hill-shadowed valley of the Shelf Brook, beneath a world of bleak gritstone moors and picturesque cloughs, Bagshawe was to exercise his ministry for some eleven years.

The ancient parish of Glossop was one of the most extensive in the north of England. The people under Bagshawe's charge lived as far apart as Salter's Bridge, near the Yorkshire border, and Marple Bridge, on the Cheshire boundary, while from north to south the parish extended from Woodhead to Chapel-en-le-Frith. All told, the area embraced by the parish boundary was approximately fifty thousand acres.

Ecclesiastically, the dependent chapelries of Charlesworth, Mellor and Hayfield belonged to the parish. When the Parliamentary Commissioners visited Glossop in 1650, they reported that the vicarage was worth £30, but had an augmentation of £50, paid out of the impropriate tithes of the Royalist Countess of Arundel, whose estates were under sequestration.

The eleven years during which Bagshawe resided at Glossop laid the foundations of his subsequent ministerial success, yet on first appearances the widest gulf seemed to stand between the new pastor and his parishioners. Born and bred in a princely hall, accustomed to expensive clothing and rich fare, able to read three languages beside his own, Bagshawe at the age of twenty-three typified the educated Christian gentleman of his day. By contrast, the manners of his people were coarse and unrefined, and their diet of rye-bread, cheese and ale was extremely simple; as to language, their only fluency lay in the Peakland dialect, colourfully expressed in the jargon of the lead-mines and the homespun repartee of the spinning-wheel. The obstacles which seemed to stand in the way of communication appeared formidable. But Bagshawe was not as remote from these hardy children of nature as we might suppose. Long experience at his father's side of the family estates had brought him into close contact with their ancient customs, insulated social habits and manner of speech. Added to this, the esteem in which his family was held in the district and his own natural affection for the people of his 'beloved Peakland' would contribute not a little to the removal of these barriers. With skilful application and help from God, the gulf could be bridged and an entrance for the Gospel secured among them.

The basis for spiritual reform in Glossop had already been laid some years earlier under the ministry of Robert Cryer, though after his departure the church had declined, either through the unregeneracy of the clergy or pastoral neglect. On surveying the parish afresh in 1651, Bagshawe judged the state of the people such that nothing less than a complete renewal of spiritual life was needed. To this end, he began to assert anew the fundamental principles of the Christian Faith. The sovereignty of God and the sinfulness of man, the righteous demands of the Law and the gracious promises of the Gospel, the impotence of human works and the necessity of faith in Christ for justification, the imperative need to show forth God's mercy in a holy life—all were faithfully declared and applied to the hearts and lives of his benighted people. The whole spectrum of revealed truth was made clear; nothing was omitted. 'I did not willingly turn aside,' he later averred, 'either to new opinions or new expressions, but asked for the old path, which is the good way, not departing from the doctrine of the Thirty-Nine Articles and the Reformed churches.' Devoid alike of subtlety in interpretation and abstruseness of language, Bagshawe's preaching consisted of a plain and practical declaration of 'the humbling doctrines of original sin; of God's exceeding grace; of imputed righteousness; and so of gratuitous justification'. That Bagshawe was second to none in his allegiance to the great doctrines of the Bible and the Reformation may be seen from the following brief extracts from his sermon notes:

'Predestination is a decree special, as distinguished from that which is general, respecting those who are chosen by and to grace, and through that to glory ...'

'The work of man's salvation is a mighty work, and of vast consequence. Are not all the Persons in the all-blessed Trinity engaged in it? and is not the new creature most noble, proceeding from the Father's purpose, the Son's purchase, and the Spirit's power?'

'I am of the opinion of those who hold that most sins take their rise from men's not believing thoroughly that ALL-SUFFICIENCY is rightly attributed to God. . . . No rest should any take till, through an all-sufficient Saviour, His Father's all-sufficiency be for them, and they for giving Him the honour of it!'

'If ever you are truly convinced that your sins have been committed against the Lord of Hosts, you will be further convinced that no righteousness which you can call your own will answer for that unrighteousness which you have been guilty of. If people wish to rest on their own righteousness, it must be perfect; faultless in the balance of God's law; infinite in its satisfaction of divine justice. Your unrighteousness makes you need Christ; your own righteousness, if set up in Christ's place, makes you incapable of benefit by the righteousness of God. . . . Christ's righteousness is (1) every way complete, answering the requirements of the law; (2) a righteousness which cannot be lost, as was Adam's; (3) a righteousness which will reach all believers.'

'There is such a privilege as being clothed with the sun of righteousness, and having the righteousness of Christ imputed. O that I may have, as well as hear of that rich clothing! May I so see my nakedness that I may hunger and thirst after it.'

'Is not justifying faith an emptied, open, clasping, active hand?'

It need not surprise us that men were immediately struck by the fervour and earnestness of their new young pastor's preaching. 'He spoke like a man who felt what he said, and had a powerful sense upon his own mind of those things which he urged on others,' noted a contemporary. God, sin and Christ; death and judgement; the torments of hell and the blessedness of heaven, were all tremendous realities to him. 'O what a fearful thing it will be,' runs his own testimony, 'for those to be condemned who had a Saviour and salvation freely offered them.'

Springing from this lively awareness of the reality of eternal things was Bagshawe's belief that the preaching of the Word of

God must be followed up by catechetical teaching and the encouragement of family prayer and Bible study. Consequently, at the same time that Richard Baxter was reaping fruit for God at Kidderminster by the same means, he commenced systematic visitation of his flock. On entering their homes, Bagshawe 'commended them to the divine compassion', and before he left gave each member of the household, young and old, his blessing. Between times, he 'assisted them in the noble work of praise', prepared them for the forthcoming Lord's Day with a seasonable address, catechised their children and freely discussed with them their everyday problems. One who later accompanied him on his pastoral rounds noticed that 'though he would be cheerful . . . to wipe off the reproach some fasten on religion, that it makes men melancholy and morose, . . . his discourse was never light and vain'. By his gentle and winning approach as much as by the truth and relevance of his teaching, his cautious parishioners were soon led to appreciate the good their new pastor wished them, and before long both he and the glad tidings he bore gained a ready entrance into their hearts.

Nor were Bagshawe's ministrations exclusively spiritual. Few men lived further than he from the popular misconception of the Puritan as a pious eccentric whose religious exercises were divorced from the harsh realities of life. Possessed of a regenerated social conscience, his bountiful eye extended to the needs of the poor of his parish. The distress of widows and orphans he relieved out of his own pocket; he procured work for the slothful and indigent. He took pains to deal out money for bread to the hungry and for clothing to the ill-clad, and invariably his almsgiving was accompanied by spiritual counsel.

A further feature of Bagshawe's public ministry at Glossop was his keen interest in the civil affairs of the parish, mainly with a view to improving public facilities and fostering social justice. This concern for public righteousness and well-being is illustrated by a petition he signed, along with twenty-seven other influential members of the parish, on December 26th, 1651, begging the Parliamentary Commissioners to continue a salary of £10 per annum paid by the late Earl of Arundel for the maintenance of a schoolmaster at Glossop Grammar School. Bagshawe's eagerness to promote sound learning in the town received a curt rebuff when the County Committee, to whom the petition had been referred, certified that the £10 had come from the estate of the Countess, who had issued instructions for payment to be stopped.

Bagshawe's influence on the town went beyond the confines of the pulpit and the under-privileged. He quickly became noted for his zeal against 'open wickedness'. On his course round the parish, he would pause to issue a word of admonition to those who profaned the Lord's Day or were guilty of gambling or ill-treating others. Discovering a group of weavers throwing dice for money, he would boldly remonstrate with them, leaving their ears ringing with the warning: 'It is not for those to play, who have wrath hanging over them.' Similarly, when he stumbled across parties of men and women dancing together on the local green or in the fields nearby, he would stop his horse and solemnly inquire whether their dancing sprang from a sincere love to God, or whether it was merely the expression of a 'vain heart'. He would remind them how much vice mixed dancing had nourished and exhort them to live lives consistent with Christian gravity. Idleness, filthy language, swearing and drunkenness were all laid open to attack from the pastor who longed to see the purity of Christ manifest in his people.

The thoroughness with which Bagshawe launched himself into the work of reforming the parish of Glossop did not cause him to neglect his own spiritual health. He was pre-eminently a man who made thorough work of his own calling and election before seeking, by God's grace, to change others. In the first place, he was a man of prayer. An early riser, he spent an hour at the throne of grace while the rest of his family slept on, and throughout each day he set aside, like the prophet Daniel, stated times for communion with God. He is said by a contemporary to have excelled in 'the special gift of prayer'. 'With holy fervour,' it was observed, 'and in very significant words, he represented to God the case of his own flock, and of the churches of Christ, and with the most powerful arguments enforced his requests on their behalf. Like a true son of Jacob, he wrestled with God and prevailed.'

It is not surprising that having been rendered deeply conscious of his own sinfulness and weakness in the sight of Him before whom the very heavens are unclean, Bagshawe was humble before others. In his dealings with those who were far inferior to himself in breeding, intellect and Christian graces, he spoke and acted as their equal. The way in which he accommodated himself to the meaner capacities of his congregation led a contemporary minister to remark that 'they were certainly as happy in a minister as any people I ever knew'. Whenever they expressed views conflicting with his own, 'he was so far from stiffness in maintaining his own sentiments, that he would calmly hear their reasonings . . . and own himself satisfied with them on their convictive clearness'. His own family noticed how severely he would reprove himself for what many would account slight defects and failures: any 'sharp words' spoken either in his own or others' houses caused him a smarting sense of grief. Bagshawe's humility showed itself too in the plainness of his speech. Apart from such terms as 'justification' and 'propitiation', which need to be understood for a proper grasp of biblical truth, he eschewed long words in favour of a pithy, candid and racy style which was peculiarly adapted to bring the great mysteries of God down to the level of his uneducated parishioners.

When people crossed the threshold of Bagshawe's home, they sensed the 'reign of grace and the power of godliness'. Family prayer and Bible study, far from being an additional 'extra' to domestic life, was its very foundation. Towards the end of Bagshawe's stay in Glossop, after two sons (John, born January 8th, 1654, and Samuel, born December 31st, 1656) had been added to the household, it must have been a rare pleasure for visitors to share the spiritual fragrance which permeated the young pastor's home. We can imagine the scene as, at the close of each day, Bagshawe exhorted those under his care from the pages of divine truth. 'Was the world or church ever blessed with such a pattern of humility as the Lord Jesus Christ was?' he meditated. 'Did ever any stoop to such a degree as He stooped? When he would have others to learn lowliness of Him, it is noted that the Greek word falls as low as the pavement. Was not His whole life a state and course of humility? and that both in reference to God His Father and to men and women His children? and is not humility said to be the essence of Christianity?' Such was the fountain from which Bagshawe and his wife drew their strength.

It may have been a later date to which John Ashe, Bagshawe's biographer, referred when he wrote that Bagshawe continued to honour his parents after raising children of his own, but the fact is noteworthy. Doubtless both he and his wife sought the counsel of his father and stepmother on important matters, besides attending them in times of illness and on family occasions, and sharing with them, in the rare moments when his heavy commitments left him free, the rugged beauties of the Peakland scenery.

When operating in combination, these factors—Bagshawe's fervent proclamation of the evangel of salvation on the sole authority of the Word of God, his careful attention to the poor and profane of his parish, his concern for social improvement and his own irreproachable example—began through the Spirit's efficacy to produce effects of great consequence upon the people of Glossop. A new seriousness about the things of eternity set in among them, and many became gripped for the first time by an urgent concern for the welfare of their souls. A spirit of contrition for sin and of longing for the peace of forgiveness and reconciliation with God troubled them. The little chapel on the hill became full of 'anxious inquirers', and Bagshawe's pastoral visits must have doubled under the strain of the situation. One such conversation that seems to date from this period was later incorporated with Bagshawe's private notes. It serves to point the nature of the struggles which many of his congregation underwent at this time. An old man, clearly awakened to a view of his sin and the righteous judgement of God by Bagshawe's sermon on Isaiah 33 : 14, came to his pastor in deep distress of soul: 'O that stinging word ever! ever! ever!' he cried, 'when applied to torturing pains, joined with the loss of heaven, and of every smile of the face of God! Many times have I disputed about the place of hell, but not until now would I shun the ways that lead down to hell. What will become of me?'

'Even if you had many souls,' replied Bagshawe, 'you ought not to have ventured on a death-bed repentance. But I tell you from God that though late repentance be seldom true, true repentance is never too late. Some came into the vineyard only at the eleventh hour, and yet they were received. . . . Jesus Christ excepts no thirsty souls from the benefits of His grace.'

'Oh, but I have rebelled against the Lord many years!'

'Here is matter for humiliation, not for desperation. The Lord Jesus Christ has received gifts—even the gifts of grace, and He is ready to bestow them on the rebellious also.'

'Oh, but my name is Backslider, I have dealt very ill with the Lord!'

'I confess that falls are dangerous, and falling backward specially so, but the Lord says, "Turn, O backsliding children"; and what follows? . . . "for I am married to you".'

'Oh, but my sins are multitudes, multitudes. What will become of me?'

'Know this, that it is as easy with God to pardon multitudes of sins as one sin. If you say that your sins are as "mountains", on your receiving Christ they shall be cast into the depths of the sea, and the sea has depths to cover the greatest mountains.'

Doubtless many conversations of this kind took place in the weavers' and shepherds' cottages that clustered around Glossop Hill, until the wondrous acts of God's love found a fresh place in those rude homes.

Such was the esteem in which Bagshawe came to be held in the High Peak that by the time of his twenty-sixth birthday his counsel was sought by Presbyterian ministers further afield. On March 20th, 1654, he was voted assistant to the Classical Assembly representing the Hundred of the Low Peak, which met at Wirksworth. At the next meeting of the Classis, on April 17th, he appeared before the presbytery and preached an 'orthodox and seasonable sermon', which was 'well approved', thereby qualifying to add his name to the list of Low Peak ministers. From then until the Restoration he played an important part in the affairs of the Low Peak churches, taking his turn in delivering the monthly 'lecture', examining candidates for the ministry and helping to solve such problems as the administration of the Lord's Supper to non-parishioners and the relief of the widows and orphans of deceased ministers.

One particular example affords us a brief glimpse at the nature of his work as a classis member. On the day following his appointment to the assembly he played a prominent role in the ordination of Anthony Buxton, who had received a call to the pastorate at Hayfield, a dependent chapelry in Bagshawe's parish. His part in the proceedings was to write Buxton's testimonial, recommending him for his 'godly conversaton' and 'orthodox judgement, faithful and painfull in the work of the Ministry', and to satisfy the presbytery that 'no exception against him' could be found among the Hayfield congregation. Upon Buxton's successful examination, Bagshawe and his colleagues the following day proclaimed him a 'tried and approved' minister of the Gospel 'by the laying on of hands'.

Towards the end of his pastorate at Glossop, Bagshawe was invited to assist the presbyters of the Manchester Classis, and on July 13th, 1658, he preached his first sermon to them. Apparently the Presbyterians of Manchester were at this time under heavy fire from both Anglican and Independent quarters. The latter in particular were making strenuous efforts to prevent the operation of the Presbyterian system on the ground that Presbyterians usurp the authority of Christ over independent congregations. Doubtless Bagshawe's conciliatory spirit and shrewd understanding of the issues involved made him an obvious choice as an additional member of the classis. At any rate, he is said to have had a hand in the controversy and in the reply the Presbyterians published to the Independent objections to their proceedings.

We must not imagine that everything ran smoothly for Bagshawe during the eleven years of his ministry at Glossop. Both personal bereavement and public opposition faced him on a number of occasions. Joyful activity first gave way to quiet resignation early in 1653, when his wife gave birth to a stillborn child. The parish register baldly refers to the event in the following terms: '1652(3) Jan. 25. Infans W. Bagshawe Vicarii de Glossope (buried).'

In 1656 the early death of Anthony Buxton, Bagshawe's closest friend, deeply affected him. Buxton, who was by that time in the living of Tideswell, fell from his horse and suffered serious injury one day while making the rounds of his parish. Shortly afterwards he died. Bagshawe was away from home when the tragic news reached him, but was able to return for the funeral. 'Alas,' he wrote, 'I who was called to lay my hands upon him (when he was ordained) was called to lay my shoulder to his bier.' At the request of the dead man's relatives, Bagshawe preached his funeral sermon, taking for his text: 'Of whom the world was not worthy' (Hebrews 11 : 38). Forty-six years later, Bagshawe shared with some old believers their memories of Buxton's brief but effectual ministry, both having retained their impressions 'of the precious truths which with much exactness he delivered'.

That Bagshawe also encountered public opposition at Glossop need not surprise those who have read the history of his times. The new Presbyterianism was constantly under attack from all quarters: defeated Royalist Anglicans, proscribed Roman Catholics, and, what in those days were called 'sectaries', all agreed in condemning their common foe.

Their motives, however, were by no means the same. Royalists, whether Anglican or Roman Catholic, were grieved that the policy of the 'Rump' Parliament for restoring the nation's economic stability after the civil wars was being implemented at their cost. Heavy excise and property taxes, and large-scale confiscations of land, supplied the adherents of the new régime with an easy way to prosperity, they claimed. Bagshawe probably shared the odium which became attached to his father at this period for buying the sequestered manorial estates of Great Hucklow for a mere £130.

There were others belonging to these parties, Bagshawe noted, whose antagonism sprang from a different source. The Parliament which now controlled the country was deeply concerned at everything which gave licence to carnality and sensuality. When the new laws against adultery, drunkenness and swearing came into force, when traditional religious feast-days were replaced by a monthly fast, when the celebration of Christmas was prohibited, when maypoles were hewn down and an effective stop was put to cock-fighting, bear-baiting and other sports, the word 'Puritan' became a term of abuse to be bandied about by the callous mob, and many longed for a return of the old ways.

Of the 'sectaries', the Quakers and the Anabaptists were the most troublesome. Outcasts under the Monarchy and Commonwealth alike, they sought to make matters as unpleasant as they dare for the new race of presbyters, whom they regarded with Milton as 'old priests writ large'. In nearby Hayfield, their 'malignancie' against Christopher Fisher, Bagshawe's assistant, was so persistent in its attempts to 'undoe, discharge and bannish' him that he was compelled to petition the Derbyshire justices to take out a warrant for their arrest. Over at Peak Forest, too, local skirmishes between Quakers and the incumbent's supporters were frequently the cause of each other's 'lamentable bruising . . . and unChristian usage'.

While such disturbances threatened the good relationships Bagshawe was seeking to develop in his parish, difficulties of another nature pressed at his door. These respected the sacraments. The evidence strongly suggests that Bagshawe found himself compelled to exercise spiritual discipline on some of his parishioners. Between 1653 and 1659, of one hundred and sixty-nine births recorded in the parish register, no more than forty-five proceeded to baptism. Now since the infant mortality rate fell far short of the discrepancy between the number of births and the number of baptisms, the conclusion is forced upon us that either a large number of anti-Puritan families refused to bring their children to Bagshawe for baptism, or that Bagshawe refused the ordinance to the children of unbelievers. Of the two suggestions, the second is the more likely, firstly because Anglicans regarded baptism as too important a rite to neglect, and secondly because Bagshawe's convictions on the subject were such as would lead him to exclude all who could in his judgement lay no claim to the covenant of Grace. Following Calvin, he saw baptism not as a regenerating means of grace to unbelievers and their children but as an aid to the faith of believers and their children. Baptism, he claimed, serves to remind the people of God that He is a covenant-keeping God. The sign or symbol of water is imposed on them as a seal that God will always be faithful to His covenant promises. All who make their covenant with Him in baptism may rely upon Him for their fulfilment. But only believers and their children are embraced by the covenant promises and blessings. It is not for strangers to partake of its ordinances. Unbelievers and their children must therefore be refused admission to the baptismal font.

A further probable source of contention respecting baptism was Bagshawe's insistence that all baptisms should be public. Though salvation is personal, he argued, it is not private, being part of God's all-embracing scheme to gather in His covenant people. By receiving public baptism, the baptised person both bore witness to God's faithfulness and became the subject of the congregation's prayers. Furthermore, the ordinance only assumes significance when springing from and accompanied by the preaching of the Word of God. For this reason, Bagshawe invariably preceded his baptisings by a sermon, dealing with 'the subjects, the duties, the blessings, and the seals of the Gospel covenant'. We can easily see why the advocates of baptismal regeneration were reluctant to bring their children to him for baptism, and why, if they did, they were turned away.

Bagshawe's practice with regard to the Lord's Supper was likewise calculated to stir up the enmity of those who trusted to their outward practice of religion. He refused to admit to the 'sacred feast' the 'grossly ignorant and notoriously profane'. Individual visitation and catechising had brought to the fore the neglected truth that many who lacked a personal faith in Christ had been hiding under their attendance at the Lord's Table. When unable to give a reason for the faith they professed, they were reckoned unworthy to partake of the sacrament and were accordingly excluded. It is noteworthy in this context, however, that he told a fellow minister that he 'durst not exclude those in whom he saw anything of the image of Christ', notwithstanding their aversion to Presbyterianism as a form of church government.

In the midst of his pressing ministerial duties, Bagshawe must have reflected on the turning tide of national events. Cromwell's New Model Army had long since crushed all Royalist opposition, and Charles had been sent to the block, an event which caused Bagshawe great grief. The bloody campaign in Ireland and the defeat of Prince Charles's forces at Worcester had effectively established the Protector as a terror to evil-doers both at home and abroad. Parliament, comprising an overwhelming number of Independents, was effectively encouraging righteous living and punishing wickedness. The controlling factors pointed to religious progress and economic stability. Jews were admitted into the country for the first time in four hundred years; Cromwell had made proposals for the formation of a European Protestant League in 1654, and a year later had authorised a nation-wide collection for the persecuted Christians of Piedmont. All these factors were symptomatic of the reforming spirit which had taken hold of the high places of the land. For his part, Bagshawe's labours had been rewarded with many conversions and, having refused several offers of preferment, he had witnessed the growth of a deep bond between himself and his 'beloved people'.

This fruitful first period of Bagshawe's ministry became seriously threatened by 1660. On the death of Cromwell, his son Richard, whom he had nominated his successor as Lord Protector, showed during his brief tenure of office that he lacked the force and capacity required of a ruler, and by an almost 'universal passion', to use Sir Winston Churchill's telling phrase, the restoration of the monarchy was demanded. When the late King's son, who had been widely referred to during the Commonwealth and the Protectorate as Charles II, 'came into his own again' in May, 1660, Bagshawe and other moderate Presbyterians never suspected that the end of the reign of the Bible in the Church was approaching. The new King's promises of a religious settlement, acceptable to Anglicans and Presbyterians alike, augured well, and Bagshawe was probably as optimistic as any of his party. It was, in fact, the unrealistic hopes of the moderate Presbyterians headed by Richard Baxter which blinded them to the oft-quoted prophecy of John Livingstone, a Scottish minister among the party escorting the new King from Holland, that they were 'bringing God's heavy wrath to Britain'.

The nation was not required to wait long for Charles to reveal his sentiments. Immediately after his coronation the statutes of the Commonwealth and Protectorate were abrogated. The zeal of the 'Cavalier' Parliament, which included a substantial number of Laudians returned from exile, was bent on crushing all religious groups out of sympathy with episcopalianism. The 'national church' was to be reframed according to the Prayer Book and episcopal government. Throughout the country, Presbyterians, Independents and Baptists were silenced in favour of re-instated Anglicans. By the early months of 1661, the old system had infiltrated into the remotest parishes of the land, and many who saw the way matters were swinging voluntarily gave up their livings. The situation grew tenser from the circumstances surrounding the Savoy Conference. While Anglicans and Presbyterians were apparently seeking to hammer out a settlement on equal terms, Convocation, the 'legal synod in England', was called to reframe ecclesiastical canons in the interests of the bishops. Meanwhile, Clarendon, the King's adviser, recommended the utmost severity against 'seditious preachers'. Before the year was out a series of bills, designed to extirpate every form of dissent from the Anglican position, was carried through. The Solemn League and Covenant was publicly burnt; seats were secured in the House of Lords for members of the episcopal bench; all members of corporations were required to take the oath of Royal Supremacy and receive communion according to Anglican practice. All municipal office was thus to be confined to Royalist Anglicans. By this time, Bagshawe and his fellow Presbyterians must have been aware that the end of their official ministry was near. Their fears were no doubt confirmed when the completion of the revised Prayer Book, made 'more grievous' to the Puritans 'than before', was announced. This widespread episcopal activity was but the prelude to the notorious Act of Uniformity.

6

Black Bartholomew (1662)

'That black Day of Bartholomew, in '62, when many pastors (and people) knew (to their sorrow) what it was to be separated from their hearers.'
(Bagshawe)

The Act of Uniformity was so framed that only a small proportion of Puritans in the country felt they could remain ministers within the 'Established Church' without violating their conscience. Acceptance of all the contents of the newly-revised Prayer Book was insisted on; ministers who had not received ordination at the hands of an Anglican bishop were discountenanced; all were to acknowledge the supreme authority of the King in both Church and State.

From May 19th to August 24th, 1662, the period between the passing of the Act and its enforcement, Bagshawe pondered the issues with which it dealt, giving them his 'maturest deliberation' and subjecting them to the 'exactest inquiries'. The considerations that weighed most heavily with him at this critical hour found expression in the written soliloquy on Ecclesiastes 7 : 14 of his 'worthy brother', John Oldfield of Carsington. Oldfield spoke as much for Bagshawe as for himself when he wrote: 'It is not, O my soul, a light matter thou art now employed in; it is not thy maintenance, family, wife and children, that are the main things considerable in this enquiry. Forget these, till thou art come to a resolution on the main business—It is, O my soul, the glory of God; the credit and advantage of religion; the good of that poor flock committed to thy keeping by the Holy Ghost; thy ministry, thy conscience, thy salvation and the salvation of others, that must cast the scale, and determine thy resolutions.'

Bagshawe resolved to pursue these considerations to their conclusion, whatever the cost to himself. Nevertheless, as a safeguard against self-deception, he did not refuse the opportunity to seek the opinions of his fellow ministers in the High Peak. Anthony Mellor, the humble curate of Taddington and a consistent Anglican for many years, was all for conforming. So too was Samuel Cryer of Castleton. That John Rowlandson, the venerable vicar of Bakewell, shared their sentiments probably struck his former pupil as strangely inconsistent. During the Commonwealth, Rowlandson had 'spoken much' against the Common Prayer Book and the ceremonies in it 'commanded by men to be used', but immediately prior to the implementation of the Act he became remarkably active in seeking to persuade Presbyterians to conform.

The learned Samuel Ogden, on the other hand, whose fellowship Bagshawe had enjoyed at Saddleworth and Fairfield before he had moved south to the living of Mackworth, could on no account see his way clear to comply with the Act's terms. An ardent and uncompromising Presbyterian, he urged his brethren in the strongest terms to forsake the backsliding national Church. 'The Church of England,' he protested, 'has dubious articles of faith, all the imperfect forms of prayer, all the erroneous translations of Scripture, all the unaccountable rubrics and prescriptions of the Common Prayer Book, together with the questionable ceremonies used, all which have been the scruples, scandals, and stumbling-stone of most good men in England for many scores of years!'

Bagshawe, without Ogden's vehemence, agreed. His attitude to the Prayer Book is ably demonstrated in the following thoughts culled from his private notebooks:

'Did the Apostles compose or impose a form for public prayers? Is there any evidence that the Lord's Prayer was used in all public and divine services? Is there not in true Church history a deep silence as to what is now named a liturgy? And are not the phrases met with in those called "fathers", concerning praying "with all their ability", "without a monitor, because from the heart", "with a regard to everyone's circumstances", "in suitable request", "with eyes closed (or elevated) and hands stretched out" significant? Should not prayers answer to providences? And can any who are not on the place understand thoroughly those (providences) which a people are under?'

Ceremonies too received a concise dismissal before the evidence of his open Bible. Were not ceremonies which received God's approval under the old dispensation of the Covenant abolished under the new, 'that there might be a gospel simplicity and plainness in His worship?' he asks. Ceremonies, he continues, pertain to actions as religious actions, while circumstances pertain to actions simply as actions. The government and discipline of the Church is impossible without circumstances, such as the time and place of worship; but to introduce ceremonies laying down 'of what cloth, and in what shape a surplice is to be made', and 'at what time, on what part, and in what manner the cross is to be used in baptism' is to burden tender consciences with Judaistic trivialia. Everything in worship must receive the explicit sanction of God's Word.

When his pro-Conformist brethren argued that additions which foster purity of worship by preserving it from corruption by the weak and unlearned are not expressly forbidden in Scripture, Bagshawe replied: 'You go too far and build too much upon negatives. Because such and such things are not expressly forbidden, are they therefore to be employed in the worship of God? and not only used, but imposed on the consciences of scruplers?' Proceeding to demonstrate from Deuteronomy 12 : 32 and 1 Corinthians 11 : 2 that not even a detail may be added to God's commands respecting worship, he asks: 'Can things be done safely, or sinlessly, which cannot be done in faith?' To this, Rowlandson, Cryer and Mellor would have replied: 'We are able to use the liturgy in faith. We have a full persuasion of mind that the ceremonies therein are lawful.' 'I see not,' answered Bagshawe, 'how such a full persuasion can be arrived at, about things for which there is not an express or virtual precept, or precedent in God's Word.' 'In this case,' their argument ran, 'a conjectural faith, that is, when we do not absolutely know that things or usages are directly contrary to the law of nature, or Scripture, is sufficient. Things of this sort may be known to be negatively consonant, or not expressly repugnant, to God's will. Besides, in using them, persons obey authority, and therein obey God.' 'Is authority authorised BY GOD,' Bagshawe inquired solemnly, 'to adjoin to His worship things of this nature? I answer, were not those who were in highest authority in the Gospel church, when they met in council (Acts 15), flatly against laying any such burdens on the church? Did they not limit their orders to THINGS NECESSARY? And did not our blessed Lord and Saviour confine His apostles to teach only the observation of such things as fell under His command and appointment? (Matthew 28 : 20). The ministers of Jesus Christ should not, by their conformity, confirm and encourage those in authority who exceed the bounds in such needless injunctions and impositions. Where variations (i.e. adjustments to the divine ordinances) have been thought small, God's displeasure hath appeared great' (1 Chronicles 15 : 13).

Bagshawe's firm belief in the binding authority of Scripture led him to similar conclusions respecting the Anglican custom of consecrating church buildings and burial grounds. The strongest warrant the Conformists produced for attaching special sanctity to such places was God's precedent of consecrating the Sanctuary. Bagshawe's incisive reply is noteworthy: 'Seeing no command or promise in the New Testament of this nature, places being only places for the service of God, not, like the Temple, of sanctity, places are now adjuncts, not parts of worship, and are immediately for the use of worshippers, not at all for the acceptableness of worship; whatever they may have of decency, they have nothing of divinity. If it be said that they render the worship more solemn, it cannot be proved that they make it more sacred. . . . The work sheds some honour on the place; the place adds no holiness to the work.'

On the topic of episcopacy, Bagshawe's voice gave no uncertain sound. From his study of the New Testament and Church history, he came to the conclusion that there were three kinds of episcopacy. The first, termed 'congregational', is where the bishop is 'overseer of a particular church or flock'; the second, designated 'presidential', is where, in a meeting of ministers and people, or synod, 'one of them, for order's sake, did guide, or moderate'; the third, unlike the other two in that it is not found in Scripture but developed after the closing of the canon, is 'diocesan or lordly episcopacy', in which one person exercises rule over several congregations and claims sole authority within his diocese in jurisdiction and ordination.

In denying the validity of this third type of episcopacy, Bagshawe employed the following arguments: such centralisation of authority as diocesan episcopacy advocates is repudiated by the biblical principle[1] that appeal should be made in cases of church discipline not 'from greater numbers to one', as would be the case if such matters were referred to the bishop alone, but 'from one to two or three, and from them to the church'. Furthermore, the Scriptures mention more than one bishop in one particular church,[2] establishing the principle of shared oversight. In any

[1] Matt. 18 : 15–17; Deut. 19 : 15.   [2] Acts 20 : 17; Titus 1 : 5; Phil. 1 : 1.

D

case, the concept of a diocese is certainly of later provenance than the New Testament. To the suggestion that episcopalianism is really no different from presbyterianism, on the ground that the terms 'bishop' and 'presbyter' are used interchangeably in the New Testament, Bagshawe replied: 'May there be a pastor of pastors, or archbishop? I answer, the Scripture mentions one archbishop, to wit, Christ. Of more I read not! Besides,' he added tantalisingly, 'can an English diocesan discharge his office in his person, or save by his chancellor, courts, etc.? and doth the Scripture favour such deputation? Is not his charge a *personal* one?'

Against England's renewal of her Erastian policy, by which the Church would again become an instrument of the State, with the King as head of both, Bagshawe took a decisive stand. While all Christians should be exemplary in their allegiance and subjection to the reigning monarch, he argued, for he is head of all subjects of the realm, both within as well as outside the Church, his authority is strictly limited to civil or secular affairs, and in no wise should he determine church policy. Rather than impose ecclesiastical laws on church members, he should 'study to magnify Christ's laws', for Christ alone is the true 'Head, King, and Law-giver of His universal church.' As soon as the King presumes to make laws which bind the conscience, he usurps Christ's Kingly office, and places himself in the position of Antichrist.

It was in this spirit of profound conviction that Bagshawe set his cause and that of the Anglicans before the tribunal of Scripture, and having done so, remained thoroughly dissatisfied with the terms of conformity the Act of 1662 offered. His living at Glossop must be vacated (despite the offer by an influential gentleman of the town to procure it for him), and, like Abraham, he must go out, 'not knowing whither he went'. He was sure, however, that by calling him to leave one sphere of usefulness, God would open up another before him, but as to its nature, he knew nothing.

Doubtless several alternatives suggested themselves to him. His father might be persuaded to allow him to throw open his rooms in Hucklow Hall as a private academy or school. Samuel Beresford, of St. Werburgh's, Derby, was planning to do this at his home in Shrewsbury. Alternatively, he could adopt the proposal of Roger Morrice, of Duffield, and pursue a life of study and literary effort, sharing with his father and two brothers the management of the family estates. Indeed, as the eldest son and rightful heir, he might consider assuming full responsibility for the Bagshawe inheritance, thereby fulfilling his father's long-cherished ambitions for him. But as he carefully reasoned with himself, Bagshawe became assured that only one line of action lay open to him: he would continue to preach the unsearchable riches of Christ. Christ alone had commissioned him to take up the care of souls; Christ alone could discharge him. At the outset of his inquiries into the clauses of the Act, he had resolved to follow only his conscience, directed by the Word of God. Now, the offer of the highest position in the land would not have swayed him to do otherwise.

When, therefore, the Feast of St. Bartholomew (August 24th) came, Bagshawe sadly bade farewell to the congregation he loved and the place where for the past eleven years he had laboured unstintingly for the conversion and edification of his people. On the eve of his departure, the building which had so frequently resounded to the evangel of salvation was filled as his sorrowful congregation gathered to hear their pastor give expression to his state of mind.

The power of this address,[1] coupled with the solemn circumstances in which it was delivered, brought the whole congregation to tears. The Apostle Paul at Ephesus received no greater token of his people's love than did Bagshawe on the occasion of Black Bartholomew.

[1] Now lost.

7

The Great Persecution (1662-72)

'Do not saints speak too much of their sufferings, whereas long-suffering is a grace of silence.'

(Bagshawe)

Immediately on his eviction from the living of Glossop, Bagshawe found his father's home generously placed at his disposal. Hucklow Hall would thus have become the centre of Protestant Non-conformity in the Peak for the remainder of the century, had not fresh circumstances transferred this privilege to Ford Hall, near Chapel-en-le-Frith.

The social status of the family had risen rapidly during the Commonwealth, the wealth it had amassed through lead-mining having been invested in property and land. A series of swift purchases in 1651 and 1652, culminating in the opportune payment of £130 for the village of Hucklow, part of the estate of the sequestered Royalist Duke of Newcastle, brought William's father new recognition as a landowner and Lord of the Manor of Hucklow. Throughout this period, however, he had continued to cast covetous eyes on Ford, which he claimed was the seat of his ancestor, Clement de la Forde, bailiff of the Royal Forest in the early 14th century. A previous opportunity to purchase the house had been missed in 1648 when the Cresswell heiress, whose inheritance it had been, sold it to a Robert Ashton of Stoney Middleton. On January 22nd, 1663, he began negotiations with Ashton for its purchase, and the conveyance was finally settled by June 30th, on the payment of £1,300. This fine Elizabethan hall, modified by the Cresswells to their 17th-century tastes, now became Bagshawe's home until his death.

Bagshawe's ejection from Glossop marks the beginning of a ministry which for its integrity, tenacity and usefulness has rarely been surpassed in the history of English pastoral work. Richard Baxter at Kidderminster, John Newton at Olney, and Murray M'Cheyne at Dundee, are each remembered as models of pastoral

42

faithfulness and distinction. In no less faithful and distinguished a way Bagshawe carried out the exacting duties of ministering to believers and evangelising over huge tracts of sparsely-inhabited Pennine moorland until he became known throughout the county and in the neighbouring counties of Cheshire and Lancashire as 'the Apostle of the Peak'. He embarked on his first itinerant tour of the wild Peak regions late in 1662, and thereafter continued without remission until the last winter of his life, some forty years later. Apart from occasional trips to Manchester, where he engaged in informal discussion with other ejected ministers respecting the lamentable change in the destiny of the Church, Bagshawe never left his 'beloved people'.

He began this 'illicit' ministry by conducting services in his father's house and at the homes of sympathetic friends nearby. With evident satisfaction, he later recalled one 'whose house in Kinder was to me and divers (who loved the truth) a little sanctuary'. As the response to his teaching enlarged, demands were made on him to exercise this private ministry outside his own immediate locality. Many of his former congregation were unable or too much afraid to make the twelve-mile journey over the moors from Glossop to Ford, but Bagshawe's heart was stirred within him as he saw all around him villages whose pulpits were now empty, their former pastors having moved to a fresh locality. Under the daily expectation of being arrested, therefore, he boldly decided to ride out on horseback and minister to their needs in person. A loosely-organised nonconformity was soon developed, although maintenance of the Presbyterian system was no longer possible, since each congregation was compelled to meet in secret and in isolation from its neighbours.

Before much time elapsed, Bagshawe's preaching ceased to be confined to the walls of private houses. Wherever he could bring people together, whether in a copse, a quarry, a barn, a field, or simply by the roadside, he was willing to teach them. No longer dependent on the offer of a pulpit, he was free to preach wherever men and women hungered for the Word of God. One such haunt of his in these early days of Nonconformity was a field on the Bank Hall estate in Chapel-en-le-Frith. Here, beneath an old tree, he would preach to large crowds of artisans, shepherds and labourers. Little wonder that the spot came to be known as 'Gospel Brow', for the gracious invitations of the Saviour rang loud and clear from the

ambassador's lips. 'Cry aloud for distinguishing grace,' he called
to the lost masses who thronged the natural amphitheatre below
him. 'It is a great encouragement to know that though you are
unworthy to receive it, the Lord is free, purely free, wholly free in
giving it. Cry mightily to God, that He would say unto you:
"Live!" Do not say against yourselves that you fear you are one of
those towards whom God has not designed to magnify His peculiar
grace. Revealed things belong to you. God has provided a
Saviour able to save to the uttermost. Come to Him. Come out of
your sins and self-confidence. Embrace the Lord Jesus and the
grace which is in and through Him.'

The meeting house on Charlesworth Hill, which remained in
Presbyterian hands after the Great Ejection under the enlightened
patronage of the Howard family, also became under Bagshawe a
well-known centre of Dissent, as did the famous barn attached to
Alport Castles Farm, beneath the wild slopes of Bleaklow. Here,
and to groups of ready listeners at Hucklow (at the home of his
brother John), Middleton-near-Youlgreave, Chelmorton, Edale
and other Peakland hamlets, Bagshawe began to exercise his ministry of the Word.

The effects of this itinerant work may partly be judged with
reference to the hamlet of Bradwell. Before 1662, its inhabitants
had worshipped in the parish church of Hope or had neglected to
worship at all. With the exception of a handful of Dissenters, some
of whom were Roman Catholics, no one evidenced sufficient
spiritual life to warrant the erection of a place of worship. The
local lead miners and farm labourers spent their leisure hours in
gambling, sometimes losing up to £10 at cards, while the religion
of those who attended worship was little more than a social exercise.
Like many other Peakland settlements, Bradwell had long lain in
spiritual death, cut off from the broader stream of English life by
its insular traditions. With Bagshawe's arrival in the autumn of
1662, the hamlet experienced a veritable awakening. His proclamation of a Saviour who justifies the most hardened but repentant
sinners aroused tremendous concern among the dissolute mining
population, and shortly, transformed men and women were
receiving him into their cottages with open arms. Frequent were
the occasions after Black Bartholomew when the voice of the
preacher and the fervent prayers of his supporters could be heard
from behind shuttered windows and bolted doors. The intensity

of the work at this period was such that before the year had expired the miners had erected a sturdy Presbyterian meeting-house, which became the first place of worship in Bradwell.

A similar pattern of events characterised the awakening throughout the whole range of Bagshawe's preaching stations. Superstitious, dissipated pagans were transformed into enlightened and serious lovers of the Bible. The spirit of fear and ignorance which hitherto had completely dominated their lives was dispelled by the Spirit of power and love and soundness of mind.

It was at this time that evangelical and dissenting interest was first fostered at Marple Bridge, on the Cheshire border. Lying adjacent to the parish boundary of Glossop, this picturesque hamlet had come under Bagshawe's plan of evangelisation for the district during his tenure of the living, but then its inhabitants showed sheer indifference to the Gospel. Still regarding himself as their rightful pastor, Bagshawe continued to visit them after his ejection. One particular autumn day in 1662, after being deeply affected by the way Bagshawe had urged them to forsake their sins and fly to the Saviour, a group of reapers in a cornfield near Smithy Lane were rehearsing the great truths they had received from him when one of them suggested they met regularly to seek God's face in prayer and Bible study. The old barn at Mill Brow was proposed as a convenient spot, whereupon they decided to convert it into a meeting-house. From that time on, throughout the entire twenty-seven years of the Great Persecution, this handful of God's people gathered under Bagshawe's ministry continued to meet undisturbed, until the Act of Toleration enabled them to register their own chapel with the authorities. The case of Marple Bridge is a striking example of God's sovereignty in salvation, for it showed that He who can bring good out of evil is not chained up by laws of parliaments and the decisions of men. The salvation He had withheld during Bagshawe's 'regular' ministry was bestowed in the period of his Nonconformity with as much ease as if the laws of the land had been completely favourable.

By the summer of 1663, the converts whom God had added to the Church since Bagshawe's ejection had joined ranks with those who had already severed their ties with the national Church to form isolated groups of believers. During the day, each pursued his occupation—ploughing the land, quarrying limestone and grit from the hills, selling clothing and kitchenware at the local markets—while Bagshawe prepared his sermons and attended to the welfare of his household. But at night, pastor and congregation would quietly wend their way across the fields and moors to some prearranged meeting spot, there to comfort and edify one another in their common faith.

'Illegal' proceedings of this nature were sufficiently extensive within the nation as a whole to provoke Charles II's government to introduce further penal measures. In May, 1664, the first Conventicle Act was passed. It stipulated that no person of sixteen years or upwards should attend any 'seditious gathering' of five or more persons, 'under pretence of religion . . . in other manner than is allowed by the liturgy'. First offenders were to be punished with up to three months' imprisonment or a £5 fine; a second offence incurred up to six months' imprisonment, and increased the fine to £10; a third or subsequent offence made the offender liable to transportation for up to seven years, including costs. If the offender escaped before transportation, or returned during the period of transportation, he was to forfeit all his land and goods. For the third offence, the offender might pay £100 in lieu of imprisonment and transportation.

Dissenters throughout the land were seriously affected by this legislation. Despite their remoteness from the capital and the forbidding nature of the Peakland terrain, Bagshawe and his scattered congregations were by no means clear of danger. Accordingly, they grew more circumspect. Times and venues of secret prayer-meetings were changed to avoid informers, and Bagshawe urged his hearers to sit under the ministry of faithful Conformists whenever they could. He himself set an example by regularly attending Anglican worship at Chapel-en-le-Frith. Every Lord's Day, morning and afternoon, he and his family ascended the cobbled hill leading to the parish church dedicated to Thomas à Becket, there to take their places alongside the lovers of the Prayer Book. This practice, begun on Bagshawe's ejection, disposed a number of influential Conformists favourably towards him. Robert Eyre of Highlow, for example, a local magistrate, refused to betray information concerning his preaching activities on account of it, thereby permitting him 'precious liberties' which were denied more extreme Dissenters.

There were few, however, who possessed the spirit of Robert Eyre. Bagshawe's enemies, caught up in the general reaction against

Puritanism which the Restoration brought, were determined to put an end to his meetings. Warrants for his arrest were issued, and petty informers proved only too ready to help bring the fugitive preacher to court. On one occasion a pair of informers, gaining prior notice of a 'conventicle', broke in on the assembly, intending to disrupt it. It is said that on seeing the awe-inspiring look Bagshawe gave them, they were both terror-stricken and fled in panic. One of them later sent for him, begging his prayers and forgiveness for his former malice. At another time, one who had sat under Bagshawe's ministry turned informer and sought to betray his former pastor. His attempts to summarise the information necessary for conviction to the local constable were so confused that the names of both people and place, and the time of their meeting, completely eluded him. To remedy the deficiency, he invented information in the hope of seeing Bagshawe arrested, but at the court sessions the presiding magistrate so fully convinced the bench of the falsehood of what the informer had sworn against Bagshawe that the charge was immediately dropped. In such ways as this, restraint was laid upon his adversaries, so that on no occasion throughout the quarter of a century of his 'illegal' ministry was Bagshawe found guilty of conventicle preaching, whereas in fact he preached thousands of times! Every Lord's Day evening found him expounding the Word to one of his congregations; 'private conferences' he managed to hold each Thursday evening with such fellow ministers as John Jones of Charlesworth and Robert Porter of Pentrich; while other evenings in the week he spent at secret services in people's homes.

During these early years of persecution, the Dissenters of the High Peak experienced the upholding grace of God in no small measure in their lives and meetings. 'The presence of God and His blessing,' claimed Samuel Ogden, 'is more abundantly experienced in our select assemblies than in the public parochial congregations.' No privation seemed too great for them. One of them Bagshawe compared to a 'labouring bee' who in zeal for the Word 'embraced every heavenly season, for the gathering of the honey of grace and knowledge'. A retired minister among them, shortly before he died at Wirksworth soon after his ejection, told the friends gathered round him that although he had been 'turned out' of his living, he was joyfully 'going to his preferment'. For his part, Bagshawe was doubly sure that he could never yield to the thought of leaving his work for some secular employment. It was in his heart both to live and to die with his Nonconformist flock. Nothing but enforced separation would cause him to forsake those with whose spiritual welfare he had been entrusted by the Holy Spirit.

In 1665, London was stricken with the Great Plague. As the number of deaths steadily increased during late summer and autumn, an 'Act for restraining Nonconformists from inhabiting Corporations', commonly known as the Five Mile Act, was being prepared. In October the Act was passed. It required all dissenting ministers to take an oath against the raising of arms in opposition to the King, on pain of exclusion from all corporate towns and any place within a radius of five miles from their centre. A penalty of £40 was attached to the breach of this clause. A further clause threatened that unless such ministers frequented 'divine service established by the laws of the Kingdom', they would incur the same fine, along with the curtailment of all their teaching activities. Thirdly, the Act insisted that Dissenters must never attempt 'at any time any alteration of government, both in Church and State'.

The first clause met with Bagshawe's ready compliance. Charles may have been both a Roman Catholic at heart and a voluptuary, yet Bagshawe's Bible taught him that the reigning sovereign was the minister of God for maintaining law and peace in the realm. That some of his laws were in direct opposition to those of Christ did not vitiate this principle.

Regarding the second clause, he had for the past three years made conscience of regular attendance at the Anglican services in Chapel-en-le-Frith, and needed no legal coercion in this respect.

The offence, however, lay in the last clause, which would manacle all dissenting ministers to the bishops' policy of 'passive obedience'. Bagshawe found this demand intolerable, for it cut across his allegiance to Christ as the sole Head of the Church. If Charles usurped the supreme authority of Christ in spiritual matters, he was to be opposed. The spheres of Caesar and of God must always remain distinct. Bagshawe preferred to endure further suffering rather than consent to an Act of Parliament which denied his Lord the prerogative of ruling His Church.

The Five Mile Act dealt a crippling blow to Bagshawe's itinerant preaching activities. Exiled from Chapel-en-le-Frith and Tideswell, and all his preaching stations within five miles of each, he was forced to seek fresh meeting places. Also he cautioned his supporters to arrange and attend meetings only with extreme care.

It was about this time that Bagshawe shared the fiery trials experienced by the Dissenters of Charlesworth and their pastor John Jones. In their protracted struggles against what has been termed the 'crowned despotism and mitred tyranny' of the Restoration years, together they wrote a glowing chapter in the history of the Church in the Peak.

Jones had never fared well at the hands of his enemies. Before the Restoration, when he was minister of a huge congregation at Marple, in Cheshire, local Royalists had silenced him for extolling the virtues of the Commonwealth and Protectorate. Having been forced into an itinerant ministry in the neighbourhood of Glossop, he was again accused in 1660 by prominent men of Mellor of disaffection to the monarchy, and was prohibited from preaching. His formal ejection two years later sealed his future as a sufferer for conscience sake. Seeking every opportunity to magnify the name of Christ, he enlarged his own house at Charlesworth to accommodate those who loved his ministry, and frequently proclaimed the Gospel there. One occasion, however, proved calamitous to him. A group of antagonistic Conformists informed the local magistrate of a proposed meeting. Barely had Jones opened his lips when the parish constable entered and arrested him. He was immediately conveyed to Chester prison, where he lay for some time in the most squalid conditions. Under pretence of seeking arms, the constable sacked the house, plundering a few harmless goods for himself in the process, and left Jones's wife and son in great distress.

Bagshawe was impotent to save his Christian brother from imprisonment, but the fine Jones's wife could not pay in her indigence for the release of her husband, he supplied from his own pocket. Furthermore, he undertook to fill the breach created by Jones's absence at the risk of following his fellow labourer to the fearsome county goal. Gaining the favour of the Howard family, the patrons of Charlesworth Chapel, he was able to exercise a valued ministry for many years among the poor shepherds and tanners of the district. After nightfall, when the howling of the wind over Charlesworth Hill and the bleating of sheep were the only sounds which broke the stillness of the scene, men and women would furtively leave their cottages in the hamlet below and ascend the hill to the ancient stone chapel. There they would await the arrival of the minister after a hazardous ten-mile journey across the moors from Ford. Numerous were the occasions when the singing of psalms and the gracious promises of the Gospel mingled with the voice of nature outside. Frequent, too, were the emergencies when the most athletic men of the village, strategically posted around the foot of the hill with lanterns, burst in on the services to give warning of the approach of the constable's lackeys, enabling Bagshawe to escape into the darkness.

Meanwhile, deprivations of another kind were reducing the village of Eyam, where Bagshawe's friend Thomas Stanley was curate, to a veritable mortuary. About the beginning of September, 1665, a box of textiles infected by the plague arrived from London, and the terrible toll on the villagers began. By October of the following year, when all signs of infection disappeared as suddenly as they arrived, seventy-six families had been visited and 260 people had succumbed to the disease. Throughout most of this period all communication between Stanley and Bagshawe and the congregation at Ashford, to which they both ministered, was severed. No one dared venture near the desolate scene, nor were Bagshawe and his people able to do more than offer prayer for the lifting of what they considered the sore hand of divine judgement from the afflicted village.

The worst of the plague was over when, in September, 1666, the Great Fire swept across the tormented capital. Two major disasters in consecutive years were regarded by many as direct visitations of divine wrath upon the immorality of Charles's reign, and especially that of his court. News of heavy losses in the Dutch War, begun a year later, was received as a further token of God's displeasure. To the persecuted Dissenters of the Peak, the continued callousness of Charles's bishops drew comparisons with the hardened heart of Pharaoh, and many wondered whether the hand of chastisement would ever be withdrawn.

Meanwhile, Bagshawe pressed on with the work of evangelisation. Previously detained within the boundary of his own parish, he was now called by the leadings of providence to sow the Word of God in nooks and corners of the Peak District where the Gospel was completely unknown. One such isolated spot was the township of Tintwistle in Longdendale. The whole valley was, in the mid-17th century, thickly studded with farmsteads. Bridle bridges were few and roads non-existent. Sheep-walks and footpaths provided the main routes from one farm to another. A dense undergrowth of bushes and trees extended over almost the entire area from Mottram to Woodhead, a distance of ten miles. The local inhabitants maintained their existence in virtual independence of the outside world, growing their own food and weaving their own clothing. Few places in England were so remote from the national scene.

To these hardy sons of nature Bagshawe first took the Gospel in 1668. During the summer months he embarked on a systematic preaching mission, visiting each cottage and farmstead, until a congregation of faithful hearers gathered themselves under one roof to form a church. For the next twenty years, before toleration gave them freedom to license a converted barn as a chapel, the people of God at Tintwistle met behind locked doors, cautiously stationing scouts at convenient signal posts throughout the valley on the lookout for approaching informers.

Bagshawe's hopes for toleration were raised during these years immediately after the Great Fire, when plans for alleviating the sufferings of Nonconformists were being considered in the capital. But these came to nothing. Instead, the spring of 1670 saw the passing of the Second Conventicle Act, designed to suppress dissent 'in the most effectual manner possible'.

Attendance at a conventicle incurred the following penalties: for a first offence, a fine of 5s.; for a second offence, 10s. The preacher was to be fined £20 for a first offence; £40 for a second offence. The person in whose house the conventicle met was to be fined £50, the fine to be levied on all present if he or she was unable to pay. No person was permitted to pay more than £10 for others. Constables and magistrates were to be fined heavily if they neglected to search out such conventicles and institute prosecutions.

In addition to these fines, Nonconformists now became more easily exposed to informers, who received encouragement from the promise of a third of the fines from successful prosecutions. Described by Andrew Marvell as 'the quintessence of arbitrary malice', this Act caused more suffering to Nonconformists than any of its predecessors.

For the next two years Bagshawe admitted to having been 'driven into corners', not out of fear of the personal consequences of conviction, but in order to render his people less vulnerable to the 'severe lash' of the prevailing laws.

8

Principiis Obsta (1671)

The crisis of 1670 stirred Bagshawe into his first phase of prolonged literary activity. Confining himself during the winter to his study in Ford Hall, he prepared for publication two tracts, 'The Ready Way to Prevent Sin' and 'A Bridle for the Tongue'. Bound together under the title *Principiis Obsta* (Principles of Prevention), these expositions of Proverbs 30 : 32 and Matthew 12 : 36 are fine practical handbooks on the topics of evil thoughts and worthless conversation respectively.

The thesis of the first tract is that the earliest appearance of evil thoughts in the mind must be resolutely opposed. Our obligation to this duty, Bagshawe maintains, stems firstly from the spirituality of the Law of God—His commandments are binding on our innermost thoughts and motives as much as on our outward actions—and secondly from the alarming truth that every sinful act we commit originates in a thought.

Since, however, the unbeliever is in bondage to sin, his immediate duty is thorough repentance and faith in Christ. The best antidote to sinful thoughts in the believer, on the other hand, is meditation on the spotless purity of God in Christ.

The second tract is a denunciation of worthless conversation, with pastoral counsel for its prevention. While commending profitable recreational conversation, Bagshawe sternly condemns all spurious heavenly-mindedness, boorish discourteousness, joking, filthy talk, lying, censoriousness, swearing and blasphemy. Such talk is more than worthless; it is sin, for our tongues were given us to glorify God. 'We must not talk at random, but by rule.' Furthermore, it wastes precious time and paves the way for other sins.

Present-day readers would do well to heed Bagshawe's pastoral counsel, which includes bridling our tongues, humbling ourselves for former failures, asking friends to admonish us for vain talk, avoiding all affectation, shunning frivolous company, weighing our words carefully before we speak, laying up a store of profitable subjects for conversation and asking God to guide our lips always. 'Those whose tongues set forth God's glory here,' Bagshawe concludes, 'shall be fully fitted to sing His praises hereafter.'

The early months of 1671 were thus spent in quiet reflection and literary effort. No small proportion of his thoughts must have been occupied with his remarkable escapes from his pursuers. Charges had been levied against him, and the eye of the law had grown increasingly vigilant of his movements. He had preached to 'illegal' gatherings for almost a decade, but when and where remained a mystery to his enemies. Scattered farmhouses and cottages beneath the slopes of Kinderscout and Bleaklow; private houses in Castleton, Hucklow and Edale; the old barns at Ashford and Marple Bridge; meeting-houses at Bradwell and Charlesworth; and many another secret rendezvous of his dissenting supporters— all could have borne testimony to the effectiveness of his ministry within their walls, yet not once had he been brought to trial.

Of more concern than his own personal safety, however, was the knowledge that his labours since Black Bartholomew had not been in vain. At least a dozen churches now flourished as a direct result of his preaching, and many households in the outlying regions gave strong evidence of having embraced the evangelical message. The encroachments of both prelacy and popery had received a distinctly powerful repulse from the biblical religion which had taken deep root among the simple Peakland folk, many of whom had learnt, through regular habits of Bible-study and prayer, extended passages of Scripture with which to combat the enemy. Whatever their social meanness, there can be little doubt that the Christianity of those converted under Bagshawe's ministry was intensely 'experimental' and eminently practical in its insistence on a close walk with God and separation from worldliness. The body of men and women raised up during the first decade of his Nonconformity was to play a decisive role in the growth of the Church in North Derbyshire for a further two generations.

News from London gave Bagshawe less cause for thankfulness. It was rumoured that secret negotiations between the King and Louis XIV of France had as their purpose the reconquest of the realm for Rome. 'The King of Great Britain,' a clause later disclosed, 'being convinced of the truth of the Catholic faith, is determined to declare himself a Catholic . . . as soon as the welfare of his realm will permit.'

The rapid advance of Romanism and the increasing degeneracy of Protestantism Bagshawe is reported to have viewed 'with unspeakable regret'. In order to plead with God for the reformation of the 'guilty nation' and for the 'turning away of the judgements that have long threatened it', he not only willingly observed the 'days of humiliation' instituted by authority, but in addition kept many 'fast days' of his own. Those who lived nearest him could testify that he 'ceased not to pour out his soul in fervent supplications at the Throne of Grace for his friends, followers, for the nation, for the countries where the work of God was most discountenanced, and for all saints'. On the rare occasions when he could gather together the servants and tenants on his estates at Ford and nearby Malcoff, he proved himself as much a champion of truth as when he showed himself before God in prayer. A contemporary noticed that, in these meetings, Bagshawe displayed great earnestness in contending against the 'blasphemous fables' of Rome, warning his hearers particularly against the heresy of transubstantiation. 'It is a dangerous deceit,' he would say to them. 'Let us be well settled and established in the grounds of the Protestant doctrine. We have need to be so. This point may cost us our souls, or our lives. As one saith, "On this stone most of the martyrs died." '

Wormhill Church [considerably rebuilt] Derbyshire
[where William Bagshawe preached his first sermon]

*Carbrook Hall, where Bagshawe was private chaplain
to Sir John Bright and his family*

*Attercliffe Chapel, where Bagshawe served
as assistant minister before his call to Glossop*

Seventeenth-century cottages at Glossop beside the church

Ford Hall as Bagshawe knew it

Ford Hall today

*The first nonconformist chapel in Bradwell,
built by the local miners for Bagshawe's ministrations
immediately after the Great Ejection*

Old coach road over the hills near Buxton

*Eyam Church, where many plague
victims were buried, and where Bagshawe's friend
Thomas Stanley ministered*

*Ashford Tithe Barn, where Bagshawe
and such fellow ministers as John Oldfield
preached after the Great Ejection*

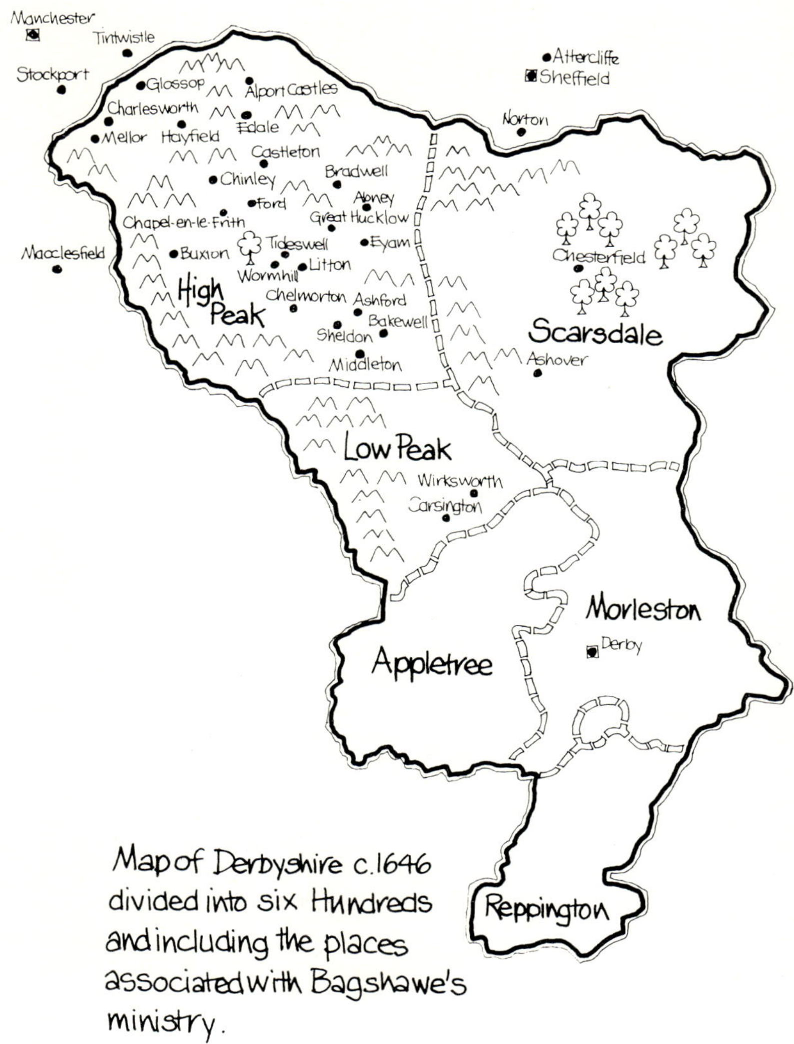

Map of Derbyshire c.1646 divided into six Hundreds and including the places associated with Bagshawe's ministry.

9

Visits of Death (1662-72)

During the first decade of the Great Persecution, Bagshawe witnessed the deaths of several people who were specially dear to him. On May 25th, 1664, four months after his tenth birthday, his eldest son John was buried in the family grave at Chapel-en-le Frith. Of the immediate cause of his death there is no record.

Five years later Bagshawe's father died. Throughout the winter of 1668–69 he showed signs of swift physical decline. Normally energetic and industrious, he was at last compelled to lay aside the oversight of his extensive estates and take to his bed. Towards the close of the following May he passed away. His decision partially to disinherit his eldest son for entering the ministry was never revoked; in his will, dated March 20th, 1667, William's legacy amounted to a third of that bequeathed to each of his brothers. Even then, his share of the inheritance remained substantial. In addition to the family seat of Ford, he received property at Malcoff, Townend, Collinhay, Brownside, Hill, Hargate Wall, Kempshill, Losehill, Green Fairfield and Tideswell. At his request, £100 of his inheritance was transferred to his sister Susannah, who would otherwise have received nothing.

On August 24th of the following year (1670), Bagshawe lost a close Christian brother by the death of 'grave, reverend and tender' Thomas Stanley. Until his refusal to observe the terms of the Corporation Act of 1661 forced him out of his living, Stanley had been the intruded rector of Eyam. After his ejection, his parishioners continued to support him by their voluntary subscriptions. During the tragic losses of 1665–66 he had shared with William Mompesson, his successor, the great responsibility of administering direction and comfort to the plague-smitten villagers.

Only a night or so before the 24th of August, Stanley was seized by a sudden illness. Suspecting it to be fatal, one of his parishioners immediately hurried to Ford and called Bagshawe from his bed. On his arrival at Eyam, Stanley confessed his faith in

Christ and rejoiced that his Lord had allowed him to suffer for conscience sake. He lingered only a short while afterwards, passing to his everlasting rest on the anniversary of Black Bartholomew.

The stringency of the laws against Nonconformity prevented Bagshawe's public officiation at Stanley's burial, but permission was granted him to preach privately to a group of relatives and friends shortly afterwards. Taking as his texts Zechariah 1 : 5 and Isaiah 57 : 1, Bagshawe enlarged on the mercy and loving-kindness of God in the death of His people. The death of the godly is occasion for joy, not sorrow, he asserted. They have finished their course and are now with their Lord. As their lives are to be highly valued while they are among us, so their deaths should bring home many lessons to our hearts when they are gone. Meditation on the inscrutable ways of God's providence should improve such occasions to our spiritual benefit. We must endeavour to see 'both the hand and the end' of the Lord in the deaths of His saints, and to 'take into our thoughts' the consequences that are likely to follow.

About a year later, in August, 1671, John Jones of Charlesworth finished his earthly course. Having encountered much opposition on account of the misrepresentation his teaching received, this venerable servant of God had spent no small part of his life suffering for conscience, culminating in the term of imprisonment at Chester already mentioned. On his release he was a broken man, emaciated by rough treatment, malnutrition and the infirmities of old age. Being invited to preach at Manchester one day in August, he was taken ill in the pulpit, and with some difficulty was brought to his own house at Charlesworth. Despite acute pain, he gave lively and serious counsel to the Christian friends at his bedside and died, only a few days later, in his seventy-second year.

The day of the burial of Bagshawe's brother-in-law, William Barber of Malcoff, was particularly memorable for the deep chord it struck in the hearts of the dead man's relatives. Following the interment, Bagshawe announced a day of humiliation for Barber's family and friends. When all were assembled, he addressed the gathering on the unexpected text of John 11 : 11, 'our friend Lazarus sleepeth'. His brother-in-law, he told them, had been a true friend of Christ: he had been included in the Covenant of Grace, he had loved his Lord and Saviour, and his life and interests had been joined with Christ's. 'He lived carefully, that he might die comfortably; and as he lived, so he died.' All Christians should likewise prepare for death by labouring in the work of the Lord, 'so to enter into His rest', by resisting and overcoming all worldly cares, and by living 'sanctified lives as justified persons. Be we much for imparted righteousness, but as to justification, plead we imputed righteousness.'

In his will, Barber had directed the sum of £82 to be paid to a 'Protestant dissenting minister residing and officiating in the parish'. Bagshawe was chosen to receive the bequest, but he gave it all to the poor.

It was not merely his deep affection for deceased relatives and friends which prompted Bagshawe to record the circumstances of their deaths so minutely. Early in his ministerial career he had noticed the extent of which people were affected by a person's death and wished to seize the opportunities for declaring the Gospel inherent in all such situations. Throughout his life he made it a matter of policy to seek out public occasions when he could address a large gathering, and his willingness to officiate at funerals thus placed him in great demand.

10

Respite (1672-73)

The early days of 1672 brought Bagshawe the encouraging news that toleration was at hand, for on March 15th King Charles signed the Declaration of Indulgence, which suspended all penal laws against Nonconformists 'in matters ecclesiastical'. The decree read as follows:

'That there be no pretence for any of our subjects to continue their illegal meetings and conventicles, Wee doe declare, that wee shall from time to time allow a sufficient number of places in all parts of this our Kingdome, for the use of such as doe not conforme to the Church of England, to meete and assemble in, in order to their publicke worship and devotion; which places shall be open and free to all persons.'

Though the wording of the Indulgence was designed to impress Charles's Protestant dissenting subjects with his magnanimity, Bagshawe, like many others, was not deceived as to its true intent. Being based on the King's claim to supremacy over the Church, a claim which carried the implication that he could reimpose fetters on Protestants whenever he chose and even authorise Romanism as the national religion, the Indulgence was to be received with great caution. Nevertheless, Bagshawe readily accepted the new opportunity to preach. He immediately petitioned for a licence and, after gaining legal recognition for the meeting-houses he required, his ministry once more assumed a regular pattern. Fortnightly engagements were commenced at Saddleworth, Charlesworth, Malcoff, Hucklow, Bradwell, Ashford, Middleton, Chelmorton, Bank End, Marple Bridge, Edale, and other centres of Noncon-formity in the north-west of the county. At Denting, or Dinting, just over the Cheshire border, he preached at the newly licensed home of William Garlicke, and on three Sundays of each month he ministered to the rapidly expanding congregation of Dissenters at Chapel-en-le-Frith. At Glossop, the place of his former ministry,

58

he renewed the monthly 'lecture' on a weekday to many members of his original congregation, who on the fourth Sunday of each month were able to sit again under his ministry. 'There, people flocked to his sermons, as doves to the windows,' commented an admirer, who noticed John Sandiforth, Bagshawe's successor in the parish, in the congregation on many occasions. Evidently he was greatly refreshed by Bagshawe's preaching after performing his own ministrations!

The nature of the unity enjoyed by these two men of God is worthy of notice. For Sandiforth, the Episcopal Church, with its Thirty-nine Articles, Homilies and Prayer Book, and its parochial system, remained the framework within which reform and evangelism could be most effectively prosecuted. Bagshawe, on the other hand, was fully convinced that Presbyterianism, with its Westminster standards, was the true New Testament form of the Church. Yet both men were deeply aware that the matters which separated them were less fundamental than the ties which bound them. Both heartily subscribed to the tenets of Calvinism; both were constrained to wrestle in prayer for their congregations; both insisted on personal holiness as the fruit of saving faith and the token of divine favour; both recognised that union with Christ, and not ordinances concerning externals, is the true foundation of the communion of saints. Genuine Christian unity exists, they asserted, where Christ by His Spirit dwells in the heart by faith.

It was not only in his relationship with Sandiforth that Bagshawe gave practical expression to Christian unity. He made a point of approaching Lawrence Brierley, vicar of Tideswell after the Ejection, with a view to their mutual benefit. Speaking of Brierley as 'one with whom I have discoursed to edification, setting aside the points wherein we differed', Bagshawe expressed pleasure 'that he was no Arminian and that he was for the due observance and sanctification of the Christian Sabbath'.

The fellowship enjoyed by Bagshawe, Sandiforth and Brierley probably did much to minimise in the High Peak the petty divisions which elsewhere prevailed between the congregations of ejected ministers and those of newly installed Anglicans.

It is evident, by the increase in the number of Presbyterian meeting-houses and the overwhelming popularity of Bagshawe's preaching at this time, that the churches of North Derbyshire were experiencing further times of refreshment from the Lord.

They had undergone many trials in the period preceding the Indulgence. Deprived by law of any building specially set apart for the worship of God except that of the parish church, they had been forced to uphold the principle of freedom of conscience by meeting surreptitiously in each others' homes, in secluded woods and under the open canopy of heaven. It was a period of great joy to them, therefore, which had in prospect the possibility of years of unmolested worship.

I I

Further Persecution (1673-83)

The period of intensive preaching activity proved to be shortlived. In February, 1673, when Parliament reassembled, a majority in the Commons, supported by an influential group in the Lords, demanded the withdrawal of the Indulgence, on the ground that only the legislature could suspend penal laws in religious matters. Under pressure from his Parliament, Charles withdrew the Indulgence on March 8th. 'All preaching licences were called in, and once more informers were sent out,' noted a wag.

The comparative freedom of the previous year was now exchanged for fifteen years of strenuous, wary living for Bagshawe and his scattered congregations. As every move of both preacher and people became subject to the close scrutiny of their enemies, the Dissenting Church again assumed the character of an underground resistance movement. During the day the artisans, cobblers, miners and shopkeepers who had received their spiritual and moral liberty through the preaching of the Word of God, worked at their respective occupations, but as soon as night shrouded the surrounding hills they would steal along the narrow country lanes and slip into some rough stone cottage, there to read the Scriptures, pray.

Bagshawe's claim to have had a 'special eye to the footsteps of Christ's flock' now received timely and practical expression in a tract entitled 'Sheet for Sufferers, or the Privilege of Passive Obedience'. Two important considerations are offered the reader in this tract. Firstly, it is not sufferers in general, nor those suffering for their own wrongdoing, but believers suffering for righteousness and a good conscience to whom 'God's glorious Spirit' offers consolation. To these alone does He minister comfort from His Word. All others, even unbelievers who share the sufferings of the true people of God in times of persecution, know nothing of that 'quiet and comfort which floweth from the hand and Spirit of God'. Secondly, all the consolation that suffering believers enjoy is grounded in their union with the Lord Jesus Christ. Their ties

with the organised Church may have been severed, but their relationship to Christ remains inviolable. However violent the storms
of the enemy, Christ will never leave His people nor forsake them.

Bagshawe's dissenting hearers stood in need of such consolation.
Between 1673 and the death of Charles II in 1685, the Derbyshire
magistrates were tenacious in tracking down conventicles and
unmitigating in their punishment of offenders. Harmless believers
were harried out of their homes, beaten and fined, and thrown
into the over-crowded county gaol alongside vicious criminals.
After 1678, when the Popish Plot stirred up officialdom against
Roman Catholic and Protestant Dissenter alike, hundreds were
convicted at the local court sessions for non-attendance at Anglican
worship. Nothing but the prevailing power of the Holy Spirit
could have kept them from exchanging the stigmas of Nonconformity for the privileges of attachment to the Establishment.

As for Bagshawe, his fortitude in face of renewed persecution
was no less apparent than his belief that on no account must the
Word of God be hindered. As in the persecution following the
martyrdom of Stephen, the Gospel was to be spread abroad, if not
by word of mouth, then by the pen of the ready writer. Accordingly, he retired to his study for long periods and commenced a
programme of patient and sustained literary effort.

His literary output during these years was prolific. In 1674, the
first part of *The Riches of Grace*, the afore-mentioned *Sheet for
Sufferers* and *Matters for Mourning* were seen through the press.
A year later, his concern for the men whose lives were spent in the
mines and quarries of the Peak found expression in *The Miner's
Monitor*. Two volumes of sermon notes (still to be seen in manuscript) were prepared in anticipation of toleration. On the '25th of
ye last month 1680/1', he commenced an exposition of the Song of
Solomon. A treatise on the Holy Spirit also dates its origin from
this period. Some 'Miscellaneous Treatises', comprising sermon
outlines, 'discourses preparatory to Sabbath Speeches at the end of
Sermons' and expository notes on Revelation 12 were begun on the
'18th of the 6th month, 1683'. An exposition of 2 Corinthians 5 : 14
entitled *The Sweetest Constraint* was penned about the same time,
while a number of small 'Treatises on Divinity', refuting the errors
of Arminianism, Antinomianism, Lutheranism, Quakerism,
Deism, and Anabaptism also found their way into his private
notebooks.

12

Riches of Grace
and Sweetest Constraint

The Riches of Grace, which occupied Bagshawe's pen intermittently between 1674 and 1683, is a fine piece of pastoral theology. Appearing as it did in the midst of persecutions, its message, that the grace of God is exceedingly rich, would have been greatly appreciated by its dissenting readers. It has, however, much more than merely contemporary value, for there has not been a generation in England for whom its teaching has no relevance. To note the leading features of Bagshawe's treatment of the subject may therefore be of value.

In the first place, Bagshawe asserts as a fundamental truth that in the salvation of God's people, divine grace in the foremost factor. Not one single stone of the building of salvation is laid by the hand of men. All is of grace. Grace is the original plan, grace in the execution of that plan and grace in its application—the entire system of salvation is undergirded, shot through and crowned with grace. If we are God's elect, it is by grace; if we are justified, it is by grace; if we have been adopted into God's family, it is by grace; if we are sanctified, it is through the riches of grace; if we enjoy comfort, it is of grace; if we enter into God's glory, that, too, is according to His grace. Grace establishes the foundation and grace lays the topmost stone.

A second feature of Bagshawe's book is the incisive way in which he thrusts aside the main opponents of the doctrines of grace in his day. He does not temporise with error and heresy, but strikes at them with the weapons of Scripture and earnestly warns his readers to avoid them. Romanism, Arminianism and Antinomianism each receive a forthright rebuttal from his pen.

Noteworthy, too, is the careful way in which Bagshawe picks his path through the intricate implications which the doctrines of grace invariably have for every believer. A fine example of this appears in the section on justification. Many believers, he says,

63

easily become confused about justification by failing to distinguish between the Romish doctrine that men are justified by *infused* righteousness and the biblical teaching that justification is by *imputed* righteousness. By believing the former, we begin to consider our own sinful works meritorious before God. This detracts from God's grace, which accepts us only for the merits of Christ's works. Similarly, he wisely cautions us to discriminate between viewing faith as the cause of our justification and faith as the means of our justification. We are justified *by* faith, not *for* it. The hand that receives a gift does not by receiving contribute one whit to its cost, nor does it render the giver less gracious. Sinners are not justified for having received Christ, but for the sake of Christ, who is received. 'He is the Gift that renders them blessed.'

Another fine passage, dealing with various teachings on holiness, is particularly applicable to the present day. It is easy to be deceived about holiness, says Bagshawe, foreseeing several modern developments. Many people confuse holiness with being civilised, with being orthodox, with a zealous outward profession, with the possession of gifts, and with temporary emotional disturbances. The true test, however, is whether God is highest in our love and whether we hate 'every false way'.

A common error about Christian comfort is also exposed and rejected. Comfort, he says, is enjoyed only by those who are holy, for 'purity fore-runs peace'. No one at peace with sin can have peace with God. A deluded notion of comfort usually makes 'large narratives of raptures and revelations', whereas true comfort springs from a humble awareness of the corruption of our natures and of 'Christ's full merit and His Father's mercy'.

Perhaps the fourth characteristic of Bagshawe's treatise which gives it a peculiar strength and value is the clear and systematic way in which he defines and opens up his topics. For example, citing the case of Jacob and Esau as the most striking instance of 'special, distinguishing grace' in the Bible, he carefully defines election by approaching it negatively; that is, he says what it is not, and then proceeds to state positively what it is. Saving grace does not 'follow blood or run in a line'—Jacob and Esau were brothers, but one was chosen, the other passed by. 'Saints become so not by their first birth but their second.' Neither does grace respect social position: they were both patriarchs, Jacob head of the Israelites and Esau of the Edomites. It was of God's 'free and sovereign disposal' that one was saved, the other reprobated. When people accuse God of being a respecter of persons, for choosing some and passing by others, he continued, they imply that He has a regard for people on account of something they are or have. But God's reasons for choosing anyone to salvation lie wholly within Himself, not in anything of merit in man. Consequently, He does no one an injustice by passing him by. Similarly, when arbitrariness is alleged against God for choosing some when all are unworthy of salvation, he replies that their very unworthiness is proof of God's electing grace. God's goodness should have led Esau to repentance, but he despised his birthright. God gave him more than he either deserved or was thankful for. Men's destruction is due to themselves. God punishes them, not arbitrarily, but for 'their sin—actual and original, deriving its origin from Adam's first transgression'. God did not make man to damn him. Just as the decree of election embraces all the means to salvation, so that of reprobation 'is not without the sight of sin'. Turning on those who would thus arraign God before their judgement-seat, he solemnly inquires, pointing them to Romans 1 : 21: 'Do you live up to the light you have?'

In similar fashion, Bagshawe neatly summarises the biblical teaching on justification. His definition is a model of conciseness. Justification, he says, is a legal transaction in which God the Supreme Judge, for the sake of Christ the Advocate, acquits man the guilty offender against his accuser the Law, thereby placing him in a relationship of favour to Himself. This legal status before God brings His people complete pardon for all their sins and acceptance as righteous before His tribunal, on the imputation of their sins to Christ and of His righteousness to them. By its very nature, therefore, justification must be the consequence of God's free favour, for no one can plead 'not guilty' before his Judge; every child of Adam stands in absolute need of forgiveness. Furthermore, believers could never be made righteous without the prior expiation of their guilt by Christ's sin-offering of Himself. God's righteous wrath needed to be propitiated before He could entertain any thoughts of reconciliation with sinful men. In addition to which, men who are dead in trespasses and sins need a divinely-bestowed faith before they can receive Christ as Mediator. And this grace gives. All, then, in a sinner's justification, is of grace.

A fifth mark of *The Riches of Grace* which deserves our attention is the strong emphasis its author lays on practical application of the truth to our own hearts and lives. Each section is rounded off by warnings and encouragements to believers and by urgent appeals to the unconverted. No reader could blame Bagshawe for mistaking himself for a believer when in fact he was an unbeliever. He spoke as plainly to the false convert as he did to the true; the distinguishing traits and duties of each were applied with equal faithfulness and force. For instance, while still expounding his subject in Book I, he breaks off to urge 'strangers to grace' to 'study the fulness of their unrighteousness and the emptiness of their own righteousness' if ever they are to be clothed with Christ's righteousness. No man will fly to Christ for covering, he says in effect, until he is thoroughly ashamed of his own filthy rags. On the other hand, 'children of grace' can discover no surer way of promoting the growth of their regenerate natures than by meditating on God's goodness and grace to themselves. Since 'all issues and events belong to Him whose grace is exceeding rich', they can be certain that their sovereign Lord commands infinite resources for their benefit and security.

Proof that Bagshawe never rested content with a mere academic consideration of his subject, but sought to stir up his readers' hearts by it, is afforded by the closing section of Book II, dealing with election. 'Let the high praises of God be in your mouths,' he exhorts the chosen seed of Jacob. 'The redeemed should continually say, "Let the Lord be magnified". Oh that their hearts and lives as well as their lips did speak the language of thankfulness!' Love God, he tells them, love the saints, and love all those 'who yet lie in their sin and misery'—this is the way to prove your election, not by wrangling over it. Then, by way of encouragement, he adds: 'He who has a peculiar favour for your persons, will give peculiar audience to your prayers; He will charge His peculiar providence with you and your concerns; He will promote you before long to distinguishing, transcending and triumphant glory.'

We notice, finally, Bagshawe's strong expression of his own personal interest in the truths he is expounding. There is nothing of the cold, clinical approach; all is life and fervour and warmth. The sins of men wring sorrow from his heart and the love of Christ draws forth his deepest joy, while frequently we find him leaving aside the main trend of his argument to engage in reverent adoration and praise.

Affixed to Part One of *The Riches of Grace* is the quaintly titled 'Matters for Mourning, or 52 Posing Proposals in order to the helping on Heart Humiliation'. Taking a verse of Scripture as his starting-point in each case, Bagshawe asks his readers fifty-two questions. The nature of the questions makes it abundantly clear that their author's purpose is to pierce through the veneer of morality which people parade as their real selves, thereby exposing their innermost thoughts and feelings to the searching light of Scripture. Man's iron mask must be torn off, and his life judged not according to the sum total of his religious observances or charitable deeds but by his relationship to God.

A sample of the questions may give the reader some idea of Bagshawe's experimental understanding of human nature: 'Hast thou set thyself as in God's sight continually, or hast thou not rather forgotten God's omnipresence, omniscience, omnipotency, and all-holiness, times without number?' 'Have the serious thoughts of the certainty of death, exactness of judgement, terror of hell, and glory of heaven, been familiar and welcome to thee?' 'Hast thou not been a frothy and filthy dreamer?' 'Hath not thine heart gathered evil from the sight of objects in themselves good?' 'Hath not guilt upon thy conscience made thee afraid to read some Scriptures, to hear some sermons, and to meditate on some great truths?' 'Hast thou been used to arguing and pleading humbly in prayer?' 'Hast thou carefully prepared for, delighted in, and made improvement of God's holy day?' 'Hast thou not heard sermons as a censurer, rather than as a trembler?' 'Canst thou bear reproofs with patience, and give them with prudence?' 'Hast thou in no case turned tempter?' By such skilfully directed arrows, Bagshawe trusted the Spirit of God to probe his readers' motives and scan the breadth of their everyday lives, thereby bringing to light such matters as require full and hearty repentance.

Bagshawe's nine sermons on 2 Corinthians 5 : 14 make some of the most heart-warming reading of his entire literary output.

The tone of these addresses is set in the introductory paragraph: 'The subject of this text is love, this love that hath all dimensions, even height and depth and breadth and length in it. It is the love of Christ . . . written in the red letters of His blood.'

Bagshawe's consideration of his subject commences with what theologians call the Covenant of Redemption: Christ's willingness in eternity to hold a 'council of grace' with His Father in which He consented to become the ransom for His people's deliverance from sin is the foundation of all His subsequent acts of love to them. This everlasting love is plainly taught in Scripture. The frequent use of such terms as 'Surety', 'Mediator' and 'Redeemer' points to a prior agreement; so do the passages which speak of the Lamb slain before the foundation of the world and the references to Christ performing His Father's will. Specific testimony is afforded by Psalm 40 : 7–8, where Christ, speaking of Himself through the Psalmist, reflects on His voluntary decision to visit earth to redeem His people.

That this eternal act of love on Christ's part was not drawn from Him by anything meritorious in His people is evident, for eternal life was given Him by the Father on their behalf before they ever existed. Furthermore, since in them by nature is 'nothing of loveliness, but much of loathesomeness', it is the love itself, not its objects, which commands our attention. We can measure the quality of this love only in so far as we appreciate that it was directed not to Christ's friends but His enemies. Not only so, the cost of His people's redemption was fully weighed before He undertook it: 'indignities, shame, pain and a curse lay fair before His eyes'.

Christ further demonstrated His love to His people by taking upon Himself their nature. Foretold in the 'protevangel' of Genesis 3 : 15, the prophecies concerning the seed of Abraham and the son of David, the Old Testament references to John the Baptist His herald, Bethlehem His birthplace, Emmanuel His name and the virginity of His mother, Christ as God incarnate is the miracle of miracles. That 'He who ceased not to be what He was should begin to be what He was not', that the Second Person of the Holy Trinity should suffer our human infirmities, that the infinite should become wedded to the finite, that the sinless One should appear in the likeness of sinful flesh—all this is evidence of the surpassing excellence of the love of Christ.

Christ's love is further seen in His work as Mediator. His giving of His own life as the ransom price for the redemption of His people is 'love, love, worthy of admiration'. God would indeed have been honoured in His justice had all been left to suffer eternal misery. How much more is He honoured, therefore, when, by His active and passive obedience, His 'doing and suffering', Christ is able to reconcile His chosen ones to their offended God and Him to them! How glorious His mediatorial work appears when, as a 'tender-hearted Friend always in court', Christ on the basis of His own meritorious righteousness restores His people to God; when as mediating Prophet He cures their ignorance of God by illuminating their minds by His Spirit in divine truth; when as Priest He cures their estrangement from God and causes their hearts to love Him: when as King He cures their impotence to obey God and subdues them to His service!

Fourthly, a special instance of Christ's love was His obedience unto death. His keeping of the entire law of God and His submission to the punishment due to breakers of that law on their behalf is the highest love imaginable. Christ's cross 'was the pulpit from whence the loudest sermon of love was preached'. Unnecessary for Himself, but indispensable to His people's salvation, the death of Christ was the outpouring of the wrath of God on Him in love for us.

Christ's death was thus a terrible punishment. God dealt with Him, not indeed as the committer of our sin, but as if He had been so. His righteous justice in all its awful weight took vengeance on sin in the person of His beloved Son. It ill becomes us to arraign our Maker for punishing the innocent on behalf of the guilty; Jesus was willing to undergo such a violent and accursed death. 'How can we think lightly or slightly of that which Christ found so heavy?'

Because it was a punishment, Christ's death was also a sacrifice; it was a religious offering in which He as our great High Priest appointed by God offered His own spotless self for the satisfaction of devine justice. 'The death of our dear Lord was a sacrifice, a proper expiatory sacrifice, yea, it was the sacrifice of sacrifices.' It was voluntary, because He freely and without compulsion offered Himself; it was propitiatory, because its aim was to pacify the wrath of God, and expiatory, because it procured the favour of God; it was acceptable, because His deity gave efficacy to the sufferings of His manhood.

Not only was Christ's death a sacrifice, it was also the payment of a ransom. Man belongs to God, but by sin he has become alienated from God. Out of sheer love, Christ contracted to reconcile him to God with the payment of His own precious life, body and soul. Jehovah, the sovereign covenant Lord whose holy law man violated, demands judicial payment for man's disobedience. But man is a captive, lying in the prison of God's wrath under the bondage of sin. Of himself he cannot pay. Christ his Redeemer therefore lays down His own life instead. 'Oh, the love of Christ our Kinsman, . . . almighty to save!'

A further special token of that love is His resurrection. 'As Christ lived and died, so He rose again with a heart full of love' and went to heaven as our Advocate, there to appear in the presence of God on behalf of His clients. We need such an Advocate for three reasons—all of us can be charged with failure and stand in need of pardon; we always have a great adversary who will never cease to accuse us; and we have innumerable petitions to put up to God. It is His excellent qualifications which render Christ a perfect Advocate—He is not ashamed to own the cause of broken-hearted sinners, His Father is sure to hear Him, He has a thorough understanding of His clients' case and He is always in court, a never-failing agent.

Last of all, His love is seen in that He is our Forerunner and Representative in heaven; He prepares a place for us, and prepares His people still on earth for heaven. All the glory we shall enjoy, and indeed that which those who went to heaven before Christ's ascension enjoy, springs from His love and merits.

In view of all these amazing tokens of love, the unconverted are to seek a thorough change of state, 'from sin to sanctity', from worldliness to godliness. And such a change must be sought at Christ's hand—sorrow for sin, hatred of sin, turning from sin, coupled with a hunger and thirst for Christ and His righteousness —all are His gifts to bestow upon His people.

Believers, on the other hand, should first meditate much on the glory that at this moment 'satisfies Christ Himself', that 'His Father from eternity purposed for them' and that 'He at the dearest rate purchased for them. It is glory in which they shall be with Him, and that for ever. Secondly, they should 'live closer to heaven'. Thirdly, they should fully familiarise themselves with thoughts of their own dissolution and departure, for they must all 'pass through the dark vault of death' that leads up to the heavenly mansions. Lastly, they should be armed by faith in their loving Saviour against all their enemies. Before you rise, he concludes in effect, as soon as you are on your feet, in all your daily work, carry around these precious thoughts of the love of Christ, and 'all along, be for keeping up a dear love to all that bear Christ's image, and a deep compassion for those that want it'.

13

Persecution Reaches its Height
(1683-88)

While the silenced preacher sat confined to his study, events of major significance to the fortunes of Nonconformity were being transacted in the national scene. In 1677, the Calvinistic William of Orange successfully negotiated marriage with the Princess Mary, daughter of the Roman Catholic Duke of York who was heir to the throne. That the greatest of religious and political enemies should become the closest relatives was a striking instance of providence. Apprehensions that England would once more become subject to a Roman Catholic dynasty had been gathering steadily during the previous months on account of Charles's renewed activities on behalf of the Papacy. The steady influx of Jesuits and other acolytes from abroad was a sure sign that the 'grim wolf of Rome' was again on the prowl. The marriage contract put an end to such apprehensions by making a Protestant succession a strong likelihood in the event of James's early death.

Nevertheless, while this event filled the national horizon, the Protestant congregations of the Peak felt the moves of Charles's active stirrings for Rome. On their doorstep at Spinkhill, a Jesuit college was actively organising its proselytising work. Priests and students, speaking the language of Protestants while seeking to undermine their faith, would have found little difficulty in gaining these simple folk for their cause had not Bagshawe and his colleagues first sown the pure Word of God among them. Their custom of learning passages of Scripture by rote under the tutelage of one of their literate brethren had admirably equipped them for the task of repulsing the enemy.

Bedevilled on one side by priests, the Reformed churches of the Peak were on the other harassed by the sects. Of these, the Quakers proved the most antagonistic. Chiefly in retaliation for their harsh treatment under the Commonwealth, they sought to redress their previous sufferings by interrupting conventicles and reporting them to the magistrates. On one occasion, in 1677, John Gratton, the well-known Derbyshire Quaker, 'rudely, arrogantly, and apparently out of pure wantonness', broke in on a meeting at Ashford while John Oldfield was preaching and disrupted the whole proceedings. No appeal could be made to the authorities owing to the illegal nature of such meetings. Gratton, who in 1662 had accused Oldfield and Bagshawe of being hirelings for leaving their flocks, showed no signs on this occasion of the unity of the Spirit for which he formerly appeared to contend so earnestly.

While similar happenings were taking place throughout the country, the discovery of the Popish Plot brought the wrath of the government on all Dissenters. In 1678, Titus Oates claimed to have exposed dark designs on the part of a group of priests to murder the King and win back the realm for Rome. In the events which followed the exposure, no discrimination was made between Roman Catholics and Protestants. The Test Act which Parliament had forced on the King in 1673 had required every commissioned officer and civil official to swear against transubstantiation and receive the sacrament according to Anglican usage. No privileges were to be given to Protestants whose allegiance to the crown was beyond question. The increasing severity with which this Act was now applied doubtless tempted many Dissenters to desert their persecuted brethren and go over to Anglicanism. To those of his congregations who might be inclined to succumb to the attractions of a privileged and respectable Conformity, Bagshawe issued the sternest warnings. 'When you are worshipping God,' he told them, 'remember that He is a jealous God, and while you live, desire always to see a warrant for whatever you use in His worship. Men may make you warrants, but they cannot put seals to them. Men may say: "I warrant you, I warrant you," but look for God's warrant.'

Between 1680 and 1685, when Nonconformist hopes fell to their lowest ebb, Bagshawe maintained a spirit of calm and faithful optimism. He refused to yield to feelings of despair, and ultimate defeat was far from his thoughts. Believing with Habakkuk of old that his enemies had been raised up by God to chastise and purify His saints, he could confidently assert with the prophet: 'Art Thou not from everlasting, O Lord my God, my Holy One? We shall not die' (Hab. 1 : 12). Indeed, it is recorded that throughout these trying years, he persistently pleaded with God for the liberty of suffering Nonconformists, and entertained a firm hope that he would see his request granted.

In this frame of mind he continued to labour incessantly for the edifying of the churches and the conversion of the lost. The following anecdote shows how much the steady increase in the number of conversions under the Great Persecution could be traced to Bagshawe's personal concern for souls. While heading for an appointed conventicle meeting, he passed the cottage of a poor shoemaker, busy at his bench. On being invited by the preacher to accompany him, the man replied: 'Ah've no time to spare. Ah've a wife and family t'keep.' At this Bagshawe inquired of him how much he could earn in an hour and a half. Having ascertained the amount, he gave the sum to the man, who thereupon accompanied him to the meeting. The next time Bagshawe was to preach there, he passed the cottage without calling. He had not proceeded far when the cobbler came running after him. Expressing surprise at seeing him, Bagshawe shrewdly asked if he could spare the time, seeing he had a wife and family to keep. In his provincial dialect, the man replied: 'Thah'll none pay mi' any more. Ah'll none stay be'ind agen. Twa' th' best money ah ever addled' [handled]. Evidently the shoemaker had received a change of heart at the first meeting and was now anxious to feed on the sincere milk of the Word!

In many such ways as this, writes a contemporary, the 'hearts of the poor were made glad by him'. Indeed, his readiness to distribute his substance to the needy, whether or not they heard the Word gladly, was so widely known that the underprivileged flocked round his horse wherever he went. Before he returned home from his preaching journeys he is said to have given away all the money he took with him!

It was about this time that Bagshawe took advantage of the informal visits he was permitted to make to members of his Nonconformist congregations who attended Anglican worship in the mornings. His shrewd opportunism led him to direct their attention to the spiritual duties of the Lord's Day. By this means he could both encourage support of faithful Conformist ministers and continue his own pastoral work. The principle he laboured to establish was 'the setting apart to God, and for His service, the day which He has set apart for Himself'. Accordingly, he directed his flock to prepare for the Lord's Day on the preceding evening by 'closing up their accounts' of the previous week with God and by seeking to bring their hearts into joyful anticipation of the blessings of the Christian Sabbath. 'Assuredly your hearts are not right with God,' he told one family, 'if you have not a holy fear lest in Sabbath services you fall short of Him and His glory.'

His custom on arriving at their homes was to give a brief formal address, followed by informal exhortations suited to the particular family he was visiting. The following extract provides an example of the latter in its expansion of one principal point:

'My dear relations,

'You who before heard of Sabbath rest, have now had some accounts of Sabbath labours; and particularly of that labour of the mind—Spiritual Meditation. I am much of opinion that the difference between a saint and an unsanctified person on the Sabbath lies not so much in any outward exercise of hearing, reading or praying, as in the inward exercise of meditating. What a man is in his thoughts, that he is in deed. Proverbs 23 : 7. Meditation is not merely a thinking, but a setting or settling of the thoughts. . . . May you show that you are renewed in the spirit of your minds by your dependence on the Spirit to influence your minds, that the day of the Lord may be begun and continued in holy meditation.'

In the years immediately preceding the death of Charles II, the persecution of Dissenters reached its peak. The records abound with exorbitant fines and the degenerate trade of petty informers. One searches in vain the annals of Derbyshire Nonconformity of the period for tokens of fair-minded consideration on the part of justices. Their relentlessness in tracking down conventicles was matched only by their cruelty in inflicting the severest punishments. At the Chesterfield Quarter Sessions of 1683, a widow, Tabitha White, was fined £20 for holding a conventicle in her home. In the same year, Samuel Ward of Allestree was fined a total of £30 5s. od. under the different clauses of the Conventicle Act: £20 for holding a conventicle in his house, £10 for permitting an unauthorised person to preach at the conventicle, and a further 5s. for being present himself! Bagshawe did not underestimate the sufferings of his brethren. He did all within his power to alleviate their burdens. He urged them to sit under the preaching of faithful Conformists; he boldly spoke up against Arminianism in local Anglican pulpits; he carefully guarded his conversation and way of life, and urged his hearers to do the same, to avoid bringing their cause into disrepute; and he undertook to pay fines for his poorer brethren. Of the latter we have an example in the case of John Whyte, of Wardlow. Whyte had been fined £20 some time in 1683 for holding a conventicle in his house. His poverty, however, prevented him from finding more than £1. After a relative had supplied a further £10, Bagshawe made up the deficiency.

How frequently Bagshawe himself was required to appear before the local magistrates is not known. Several warrants were issued for his arrest, and he must have been continually in danger of being apprehended, but how far the warrants were pursued remains a closed book. The only recorded occasion on which he was fined for attending a conventicle was on July 10th, 1683, when George Eaton, son of a prominent Cheshire minister, led the service. It speaks well of Bagshawe's modesty, comments Dr. Cox, the county historian, that he was prepared to listen to much younger and inexperienced preachers when he was probably the most gifted preacher in the county.

Some of the most fruitful work in which Bagshawe was employed during the height of persecution involved the more wealthy of the families of North Derbyshire, a class infrequently reached by the Gospel. When he was unable to preach to all and sundry, he felt entrusted with a special commission to win for Christ those in high places. His own social position thus became a valuable means of securing an entrance for the Gospel among the ranks of the cultured. Every noble household in the land, asserted Bagshawe, should be 'sometimes a court, often an academy, and always a church'. It was his constant endeavour to be instrumental in realising this high ideal. Consequently, the natural channels of blood relationship and close human friendship led him into a number of influential households at Abney, Great Hucklow, Castleton, and Chapel-en-le-Frith, as an ambassador for Christ. Like the Apostle Paul, he spent no little time ministering privately to those that were of reputation. From an improvised pulpit in apartments which had been adapted to meet his requirements, or simply occupying a prominent place in a sizeable drawing-room, Bagshawe proclaimed the doctrines of human corruption and

Divine grace with as much effect as if he were among humble miners and farm labourers. In the outcome, man's total inability to retrieve himself from a state of sin, the necessity of regeneration and of faith in the atoning work of Christ, the Divine call to holiness—doctrines usually so offensive to high rank and good breeding—were as well received among the social élite of the Peak as they had been by his parishioners at Glossop.

One of Bagshawe's most cherished resorts during these momentous times was the home of Henry Gill, cousin of Bagshawe's daughter-in-law. There, at the 'beloved Oaks', Norton, he preached regularly with much power and acceptance. A particular sermon on Psalm 25 : 21, 'Let integrity and uprightness preserve me', made a lasting impression on all who were present at its delivery. Especially memorable was the following exhortation: 'In these times of danger, it is our duty, interest, and wisdom, to get integrity, and to determine never to part with it! May we not have a thought of sinful compliance!'

The special circumstances in which Bagshawe found himself, as a Christian minister of private means, led him more than ever at this time to insist on the value of his home as a centre for prayer, Bible-study, discussion, and recreation. During the summer months of each year, either out of fearless disrespect for the prevailing laws against Nonconformists or because he had gained the confidence and esteem of local influential Anglicans to such a degree that they were reluctant to denounce his activities, Bagshawe threw open Ford Hall for such purposes to fellow ministers and students offering themselves for the Presbyterian ministry. Doctrinal, homiletical and pastoral problems were hammered out in a spirit of hope and humble dependence on God for the future. Contemporary theological controversies (such as the Socinian question), the duties of a minister, predestination, the privileges of the Covenant of Grace, temperance, and fasting, are but a few of the topics which occupied the thoughts of the dissenting clergy of North Derbyshire on these occasions.

One of the most memorable of these 'young men's conferences', as Bagshawe called them, took place in the summer of 1683, when he gave a long and searching address on the Fruits of the Holy Spirit (Gal. 5 : 22–23). The eminently practical nature of Bagshawe's ministry is evident from the following remarks, selected from his manuscript notes compiled for the conference: 'As moralists say of virtues, divines say of graces—they are as one chain, though consisting of divers links, and they are all called grace (2 Peter 3 : 18). To the same grace are several names given, according to its several workings: (1) As it causes the soul to cleave to God, it is love. (2) As it enlarges it towards Him, joy. (3) As it creates a calm in it, peace. (4) As it strengthens it to bear, long-suffering. (5) As it renders it courteous, gentleness. (6) As it makes it communicative, goodness. (7) As it brings it to and bases it on Christ, faith. (8) As it tempers and composes it, meekness. (9) As it moderates it in reference to sensuous gratification, temperance.'

'Look we among those who place their delight chiefly in some person or thing that is short of God, and see whether any of them be a close walker with Him.' On the subject of long-suffering he writes: 'Do not saints speak too much of their sufferings, whereas long-suffering is a grace of silence.' Similarly, Bagshawe's understanding of Christian meekness is anything but superficial: 'Its seat is a heart which hath been broken for sin. Its root is faith, that unites and cleaves to Christ. Its attendant is love to God, and to man on God's account. Its reference is to the honour of Him who is its Author.' Lack of meekness, he adds, is evidenced by men's rebellion against the instructions and corrections of their superiors, by their speaking roughly to their inferiors, and by their taking offence from and being 'touchy' towards their equals.

On the subject of peace, Bagshawe proves himself a skilful divider of the Word: 'The peace-ableness of the unregenerate hath no due care of (or zeal for) purity joined with it. Such can easily bear that which is, and those who are evil. They are more afraid that men should be displeased than that God should be dishonoured. They will not reprove where they have a call. But the sanctified are for following holiness with peace' (Hebrews 12 : 14).

Lastly, we quote a few sober remarks on the topic of temperance. Eating and drinking, he says, should never be permitted to prejudice health; they are 'to be used for (and not against) the body. Some long and repeated drinks are wrongly called healths. . . . It is sad when wine goes in till sense goes out!' Because drinking is for our 'necessary nourishment or convenient refreshment', we are to seek the glory of God in it, according to the comprehensive principle laid down by the apostle in 1 Corinthians 10 : 31.

Having dwelt at large on each fruit of the Spirit in particular,

Bagshawe concludes by stating that the best way to possess and express these Christian graces is to seek intimate communion with the One Who was filled with the Spirit without measure: 'The vessels are fullest of grace which are nearest its spring. The more Christ's glory is beheld, the more men are changed' (2 Cor. 3 : 18).

These seasons of prayer and study and conference at Ford Hall came to be regarded within the Nonconformist circles of North Derbyshire as times of great spiritual benefit, for Bagshawe's ministry was in every respect a character-building ministry. When young men from all over the Peak District could testify to the ways in which his mature wisdom and experience had profited them, there was never any question of discontinuing the conferences. Sometimes, for convenience, they were transferred to other centres of Dissent in the north of the county, such as Ashford and Charlesworth, but, wherever the venue, Bagshawe set aside all other duties during three weeks of each summer in order to attend them. In the closing years of his life, when natural infirmity prevented his attendance, he never failed to forward letters of counsel to the conference, and he spent much time in prayer on behalf of its members.

On April 20th, 1685, Bagshawe's sole surviving son, Samuel, who is said to have possessed much of his father's 'excellent spirit', married Sarah Child, of Holmes Hall, near Leeds. From this date, when, following 17th-century custom, Samuel brought his wife under his father's roof, management of the family estates passed into his hands. Purchases and sales of land were henceforth transacted in his name. With the arrival of his three sons, William, Samuel and Nathaniel, in 1686, 1690 and 1697 respectively, the influence of evangelical principles was secured for the family for a further generation. Indeed, not until late in the following century did William Bagshawe's direct successors cease to hold the doctrines of the Westminster Assembly. The prophecy that 'one generation shall praise thy name to another' was thus fulfilled in the Bagshawe household for over a hundred years.

The early part of 1685 also brought Bagshawe the news that Charles II had succumbed to a fatal seizure. His death brought no sigh of relief from the Dissenter's lips, only deep concern, 'having fears upon his spirit when he saw a Popish successor on the throne'. When a contemporary chronicler on the banks of the Tiber eulogised James's accession with the words: 'He gives a new day to

England; a day of joy', Bagshawe failed to share his sentiments.

James proved much more resolute than his brother Charles. Energetic, imperious and fanatical, he would stop at nothing to re-establish the rule of Rome over the nation. Were his dream of 'reconverting England to Rome under the sword of France' to be fulfilled, all the precious fruits of the Reformation would be lost, and the people once more plunged into ignorance and superstition. Almost the entire nation, vividly recalling Mary Tudor and the fires of Smithfield, feared for its freedom.

Providentially, the King's dream was denied fulfilment. Immediately after his accession, Parliament called James to enforce the law against all Dissenters, including those of his own persuasion. Popular feeling against him ran high when attention was drawn to his public practice of Romanism and when, by Louis XIV's revocation of the Edict of Nantes, all remaining Huguenot liberties were, to the accompaniment of savage persecution, ruthlessly swept away.

With the arrival at Lyme Regis from Holland of the Duke of Monmouth, it appeared to many that England's deliverer had come. His assertion of the validity of his father Charles II's marriage to his mother, Lucy Waters, and his strong denunciation of James as a usurper, strengthened public opinion in his favour. The large numbers which greeted him brought a real threat to James that all England would rise against him under the 'beloved Protestant Duke'.

It is on record that Bagshawe would have nothing to do with the Monmouth Rebellion. Ashe relates that he entertained an 'ill opinion' of it from the first, and that, true to his convictions, he was active in dissuading others in the county from supporting it. Not for the first time were his fears justified in the events which followed. A general reaction gripped the King and Parliament, the Duke was defeated in the West Country and sent to the scaffold, and hundreds of his dissenting supporters were barbarously punished by the infamous Judge Jeffreys for their misguided enthusiasm.

The alarming nature of the events which crowded into the opening months of the new King's reign, and James's excessive zeal for Romanism in particular, presented Bagshawe with a clarion call to action. 'He allowed himself but little time for sleep, and was very seldom out of his study, unless at meal times, at family worship, or when abroad on the work of the ministry' (Ashe). A series of sermons on 2 Thessalonians 2 : 3–12, designed to 'arm his people against Popery', was the result of his renewed exertions.

Bagshawe rejects the suggestions that Antichrist is to be identified with the devil incarnate, Nero revived, a Jew of the tribe of Dan, Simon Magus, the emperor Caligula, or Mahomet, and takes his stand with the main body of Reformers and Puritans in asserting that Romanism, as embodied in the Papacy, bears all the marks of the Man of Sin spoken of in Thessalonians. Daniel 7 and Revelation 17 are invoked as confirmation of this view.

His treatise is a well-informed and eminently practical attack on the entire Papal system. The pre-Reformation Reformers, such as Wycliffe and Huss, had questioned some of its abuses and occasionally the validity of the Papacy itself, but not until the 17th century, when the Inquisition and the Council of Trent and the unspeakable immorality of the Renaissance popes could be seen at a distance, was the system fully identified with the biblical Antichrist.

For the first time in his writings we find an abundance of well-directed satire. In a way particularly adapted to instil into his uneducated audiences a deep-rooted antipathy to Romanism, he is not slow to use every weapon available from his intellectual armoury—stark contrasts between the popes and the Lord Jesus Christ, stressing the vainglory and extravagance of the one and the humility and simple spiritual beauty of the other; popular broadsides such as 'The Pope claims succession from the Apostle Peter, but the text (Son of Perdition) tells us that he is the successor of the Apostle Judas!'; pathetic pleas on behalf of the poor, benighted slaves of the Papacy; and catching word-plays, for example, 'He pretends to be the apostolical friend of Christ, but he is His apostatical enemy!'; protracted arguments employing syllogisms and ridiculous processions of Rome's 'many mediators of intercession'—all add grist to the mill of this popular exposure of the 'Beast' of Revelation. The total picture which emerges is of the Papal system as a gross caricature of biblical Christianity, both doctrinally and ethically. Its mass is represented as a parody of the death of the Redeemer; its priests as play-actors; its authority (being 'magisterial, not ministerial', by the sword, not the Word; secular, not sacred) as devilish; its 'gospel' a mystery of iniquity, not godliness; and its 'god' Antichrist himself. 'Where can we find a man that hath these marks (i.e. listed in 2 Thessalonians 2) so fully as the Roman Pontiff?' he asks in horror.

No small measure of the success of these sermons can be attributed to the twin notes of victory and compassion which are sounded throughout. As the wickedness at the heart of the Papacy is being painted in the blackest colours, a broad ray of hope always shines through to calm the fears of his hearers. The ultimate doom of Rome is assured; she will be consumed by the breath of Christ's mouth. The sovereign Lord of history will in the Judgement Day mete out to the 'great whore' her due punishment. Thus victory is certain. But there is also compassion. Though the popes and their wretched followers shall certainly perish, some who have been caught up in her toils will be saved. 'A Papist as a Papist is out of the way of salvation: a Papist as a Christian may be a true penitent, and on Christ's account be pardoned.' Bagshawe's evident love for such souls, as distinct from his hatred of the religious tyranny to which they were subject, also finds expression in his concluding directions to the reader: 'May we of what has been said, make good use. (1) Pitying the servants and slaves of Rome as to the state and case of their souls. (2) Praising God so far as He has discovered (i.e. revealed or exposed) Antichrist. (3) Cleaving to that ministry in and by which Christ is exalted. (4) Looking and longing for the future and fuller revelation of Him. (5) Living down, as well as arguing down, Antichristianism. (6) Holding communion with those churches which are separated from it.'

14

The Academy (1688)

Meanwhile, in his capital city, James had taken advantage of the nation-wide rally to the crown to which the defeat of Monmouth had led. Seeking the earliest opportunity to relieve Roman Catholics of persecution, he annulled every penal law against all Nonconformists by a Declaration of Indulgence (April 4th, 1687). Bagshawe's reactions were characteristic: 'Though Mr. Bagshawe was far from owning the power of dispensation on which King James's indulgence was founded, and could not help discerning his design in it, yet he embraced the opportunity it gave him to show his zeal in his heavenly Master's service' (Ashe). On the other hand, John Bunyan, Richard Baxter and John Howe, three of his great Puritan contemporaries, refused the relief which the indulgence offered.

Bagshawe's thoughts now turned to the future of the congregations who had attended his preaching ministry during the previous twenty-five years. Some of his former hearers had been replaced by a younger generation, born in the fires of affliction and consequently overflowing with zeal, but lacking a stable sense of church order. Their energies needed to be consolidated and channelled. Presbyterianism it was clearly impossible to apply, owing to the shortage of trained ministers and the enforced autonomy of each local worshipping group. Bagshawe sought to remedy these defects by making his home a kind of Presbyterian Academy. Early in 1688 he invited Samuel Ogden, the highly-respected High Master of Wirksworth Grammar School, to take up residence at Ford Hall and to bring with him a number of young ministerial candidates. Ogden accepted the invitation, boarded the students nearby for convenience, and shared with Bagshawe the task of preparing them for ordination.

The two men divided the curriculum according to their particular gifts: Bagshawe counselled the students on homiletics and pastoral theology; Ogden, on church history, polemics and

82

'casuistical divinity'. Each morning after breakfast the young men would assemble with their tutors in the library, divide themselves into two groups and commence their studies.

The great preacher's lessons were conducted informally, in the manner of a university tutorial. On the subject of the substance of preaching, he would say: 'I am full of the belief of my betters that the strength of sermons lieth in their being scriptural and spiritual. O that what is here recommended to you were more so! . . . Let the Holy Spirit be much in your preaching. By the ill-will of the Evil Spirit, ministers seldom preach about the Holy Spirit, or their preaching savours very little of the Spirit. . . . O how hard do the best find it to live and walk in the Spirit, though to speak of so doing is easy! . . . The great themes of your ministry are to be the humbling doctrines of original sin; of God's exceeding grace; of the imputed righteousness of Jesus Christ; of regeneration. . . . Preach regeneration,' he said with great emphasis, 'preach the new birth and the new creation. As there is no salvation save by Christ, so there is no being in Christ save where there is a new creation. . . . Some will accuse you of preaching that such a new creature is nothing but a mere Puritanical and Calvinistical imagination, but heed them not! . . . Regeneration is the foundation of all communion with God.'

Bagshawe was no less practical when he spoke on the style of preaching. 'Tho' matter in a sermon is most material, yet the manner of delivering it is of no small consideration and conducibleness to people's profit.' Every preacher, he advocated, should 'get his eyes down to the people, and preach as if he were talking to people'. His address should be logically arranged, movement from one point to the next being natural and organic. John Ashe, one of the students, observed that Bagshawe's own practice in this respect was exemplary. 'The several parts of his discourses', he noticed, 'had such a connexion with, and dependence on, one another, that a diligent hearer, though of no extraordinary capacity, might retain the substance of them.'

Illustrations, Bagshawe counselled, must be apt and brief. The more closely they are related to the everyday experiences of ordinary people, the more striking they will be. For example, he continued, 'One day as I travelled over the moors towards Tideswell and Litton, I noticed three things about the local sheep. They managed to survive on little grass; they were marked; the sheep bearing the same mark grazed near one another, tho' sometimes a sheep of a different brand came among them. This taught me (1) that believers will thrive and prosper where their minister suits their state or condition, tho' he may lack many gifts and learning; (2) that Christians, as the flock of the Lord, bear His distinctive mark ... they hear His voice, follow Him ... (3) that genuine Christians have to maintain fellowship with one another in attending on the means of grace, though those of another stamp may come amongst them.'

An effective teaching method, he advocated, is to throw out to your hearers certain propositions in question form, thereby stimulating their inquiry. 'Instance the proposition: "Jesus Christ is a Christian's righteousness",' he would say. 'Your hearers will be more convinced when you ask them: "Doth not His name make this known to us?" for Jeremy the prophet calls Him "The Lord our Righteousness" (Jer. 23 : 6). Did He not as a satisfier obtain, and doth He not as an intercessor apply righteousness? (Rom. 4 : 25) and did He not fulfil all righteousness, answering for His people both the penalty and precept of the law?' (Gal. 4 : 4, 5). A striking instance of this method appears in the question Bagshawe frequently asked his own congregations: 'How can they rejoice in God's perfections, who see them not in the face of Jesus Christ?'

The young men at Ford Hall doubtless understood that they were being taught by no commonplace mentor. Not only did Bagshawe display a formidable grasp of biblical truth, he invariably directed it to the needs of the people. His claim to have 'put much of' his 'sermons into application' would serve his students as a strong incentive to imitate his good example, particularly when he proceeded to enforce the claim with specific examples such as the following: Speaking on Titus 3 : 2, he remarked: 'Christians ought to show all meekness unto all men. I was the other night more affected with this passage than ever I had been before, and sensible how far short I fell of observing this one commandment, and I fear that all of you have fallen short as to a due performance of it. Christians should not only *have* meekness, but *show* meekness, and not meekness only, but *all* meekness, not only to men of their own humour, but to *all* men, to those who have given them the greatest provocation.'

In such ways as this Bagshawe the spiritual physician instructed his students in the art of bringing the Word of God to bear on the devious ways of the human heart. Perhaps the whole range of these 'lectures' may be summarised in a fragment which appears in one of the aforementioned notebooks: 'How should ministers preach?' he enquires. 'Compassionately, plainly, experimentally, clearly, zealously, faithfully, humbly, solidly, wisely, distinguishingly, takingly, Scripturally, longingly after the conversion of the hearers,' comes the humbling reply.

By contrast with the preacher's informal manner, the experienced schoolmaster's chief method of instruction was to propose certain controversial passages of Scripture to his pupils, who were then required to give solutions in writing. The epistle of James, the seventh of Romans, the visions of Daniel and John, and such passages as would appear to favour an Arminian interpretation of Christ's redemptive work, were doubtless the centre of much animated discussion under Ogden's skilful direction. Topics such as the relationship between Law and Grace and between Faith and Works, the nature and extent of the atonement, the spiritual warfare of the Christian, and the biblical covenants, would be subjected to the most thorough inquiry on the part of his zealous students. To aid them in their work, Bagshawe generously placed his large and valuable library entirely at their disposal. Having read and marked almost every book in his collection, he was able to direct them to the best literature on the subject at hand, thereby conserving time and effort. Such foundational commentaries as those of Calvin, Poole and Trapp were supplemented by more specialised works, such as Gurnall's treatise on *The Whole Armour of God*, John Owen's *Death of Death*, Durham on the Holy Spirit, Alleine's *Alarm to the Unconverted*, and the martyrologies of Foxe and Clarke. Classical and patristic writers, notably Chrysostom and Augustine, were also available for their use.

Bagshawe's 'Academy' was confessedly an improvised affair, born of desperate need to supply the North Derbyshire pulpits with sanctified, educated men. No one was more conscious of its deficiencies than Bagshawe himself. When he heard, therefore, that the learned Richard Frankland, once selected by Cromwell to become one of the first professors of the University of Durham, had moved from Rathmell, in North Yorks, to Attercliffe, where he opened an Academy at the invitation of the influential Spencer family, he recommended his students to go to him. During the three years of Frankland's directorship of the Academy, Christ's College, as it came to be called, trained no less than fifty-one students for the ministry, some six of whom had been sent by Bagshawe. John Ashe, of Ashford, Bagshawe's nephew, was to become the most influential of the Derbyshire men; along with Dr. James Clegg he accepted responsibility for all the Peakland churches after Bagshawe's death.

15

Toleration and Reconstruction
(1689-96)

If, for Bagshawe, local prospects in and around 1688 were brighter than at any previous time in James's reign, events on the national scene also put new hope into Nonconformist hearts. By May, 1688, James's wholesale move to grant as many dispensations as possible to Roman Catholics had caused almost the whole nation to hate him. Derbyshire Protestants had keenly felt the effects of these moves by the appointment of the country's leading Roman Catholics, William Fitzherbert and Sir Henry Hunloke, as Justices of the Peace. By the 'Glorious Revolution', however, James was bloodlessly deposed and William of Orange was invited to accept the throne. The deliverer, 'clad with power from over the seas to rescue England from popery and slavery', had arrived. 'And what do you think of predestination now?' William triumphantly asked Bishop Burnet as he landed at Torbay, on being reminded that it was the anniversary of the Gunpowder Plot!

The accession of William and Mary marked the beginning of what promised to be a most auspicious reign for Church and nation. Bagshawe 'greatly rejoiced' at the event. In the capital, negotiations towards granting liberty of conscience to all Protestant Nonconformists were begun immediately. Less than a year after their coronation an Act of Toleration was passed. Protestant Dissent had at last been recognised by law. The 'Great Persecution' had ended. No longer obliged to attend Anglican services, Bagshawe and his scattered congregations could now register their own meeting-houses and continue their form of worship unmolested. Two conditions only, neither of which was grievous to them, were stipulated: firstly, they were required to swear against Roman Catholic supremacy in both Church and State; secondly, they must subscribe to the XXXIX Articles, except nos. 34–36

G   87

inclusive, concerning church traditions, the homilies, and the consecration of bishops and ministers.

Bagshawe immediately took advantage of the new-found liberty. At the Translation Sessions of 1689, along with seventeen other 'Protestant Dissenting Preachers' in the county, he took out a preaching licence and recommenced the work of consolidation which had been terminated by law sixteen years earlier. At the age of sixty-one, when most men would admit of some decline in their natural powers, Bagshawe remained as active as ever.

His first step was to obtain reissues of the licences for the meeting-houses which had been approved under the 1672 Indulgence. Where the demand for Bagshawe's ministry exceeded the financial resources available to build a meeting-house, private individuals offered buildings of their own for registration as dissenting places of worship. Bagshawe's brother John, since his father's death Lord of the Manor at Hucklow and a potent influence for good amongst the gentry of the district, was but one of many who opened their homes to lovers of the Gospel.

The licences granted, preaching engagements quickly filled Bagshawe's diary. At Malcoff, he conducted both services each Lord's Day. On three weekdays he visited his previous preaching stations, frequently addressing large crowds in several places on the same day. The remainder of his time was occupied with pastoral visits, writing books, training younger men for the ministry and visiting fellow ministers and family friends in Yorkshire and Lancashire.

The zeal he displayed in his Lord's service may in some measure be gauged by the fact that, in keen anticipation of the day of toleration, Bagshawe had drawn up during the closing years of the Great Persecution skeleton outlines of innumerable sermons. The renewed demands on him as a preacher may be thought to have exhausted his stock in a comparatively short time, yet he is said to have prepared so many addresses that a considerable number were never delivered by the time of his death, thirteen years later!

With the granting of religious freedom, the centre of Nonconformity in the Peak shifted from Ford Hall to Chapel-en-le-Frith. Outstripping both Buxton and Glossop in importance in the 17th century, this bustling market town and pack-horse link on the Sheffield to Manchester route was an ideal centre from which to propagate the Gospel. The spiritual progress of Nonconformity during the previous quarter of a century may be partly assessed from the fact that no less than 40 per cent of the yeomen of the parish had become open followers of Bagshawe's teaching by 1690.

It was upon their initiative that Chinley Chapel was built after Bagshawe's death as a memorial to their former pastor.[1]

Meanwhile, on the national scene, William III, having proclaimed a general toleration for Nonconformist Protestants (Roman Catholics, Socinians and Arians were excluded by the terms of the 1689 Act), now wished to secure for them a general comprehension. To this end, he commissioned thirty divines, ten of whom were Anglican bishops, 'to prepare such alterations of the liturgy and canons' as would 'conduce to the reconciling of differences'. The Bill proposing these alterations was, however, rejected by the Commons, upon which Presbyterians and Independents in the capital sank their old differences and formed a Union, drawing up principles which they hoped would gain the subscription of both parties throughout the country.

When a group of Presbyterian and Independent ministers from Cheshire gathered at Macclesfield in March, 1691, to consider the proposed union, Bagshawe was among them. The terms of agreement proposed in London received their initial assent, after which the United Brethren, as they called themselves, considered questions of order. At a second meeting of the confraternity (April 14th) a letter on the subject from the celebrated John Howe was read to the assembly and discussed. A further meeting was then convened at Dean Row, near Wilmslow, where 'ye agreement of ye London ministers was deliberately read over, considered, and subscribed by all'.

That Bagshawe played a leading role in these discussions is evident by the appearance of his name at the head of the list of subscribing ministers. The principles to which he and his fellow ministers, amongst whom was the illustrious Matthew Henry, subscribed, are worthy of summary:

Membership of the Church of Christ belongs only to those who are sound in biblical doctrine and faithful in their lives. Each local church must elect its own officers, who are to be ministers and

---

[1] Bagshawe's oak pulpit from Malcoff continues to be used there, having been presented to the chapel by Major F. E. G. Bagshawe in 1931 after two centuries of preservation in Ford Hall.

elders or deacons. Differences over the latter are not to cause a breach. Elected ministers are first to be called by Christ, and His calling is to be confirmed by the local congregation in conjunction with the advice of neighbouring churches. The United Brethren are to bear 'Christian respect' to their fellow Christians, to explain the doctrines and way of salvation to the 'ignorant and vicious', and to receive qualified persons into church fellowship.

On August 11th, 1691, the Cheshire Association, as the Brethren termed their Society, drew up its own rules. Meetings, presided over by a moderator, were to be held frequently, and would include prayer and a sermon followed by mutual consultation. Days of humiliation to confess their sins, their 'past differences', and 'present shortcomings', and to 'thankfully acknowledge the Lord's great goodness in agreeing and carrying them on thus far', were set apart; each minister pledged himself to direct the force of his doctrine and to exercise church discipline against the sins of his congregation; all secondary differences were to be respected but subordinated to the common purpose of deepening and extending the power of the Gospel.

The subsequent history of the Cheshire Association and similar bodies throughout the country proved that, although they achieved a structural reform and rediscovered afresh the fundamental unity of believers which had been obscured for many years, they were unable to counteract the heresies of Socianinism and Arianism which were already gnawing at the vitals of the Church. By 1740 they were a spent force, largely because the men who filled them lost sight of the original intention of the 1691 proposals—namely a return not merely to the unity but also to the purity of the Gospel Church. Tentative and imperfect though they were, the attempts of 1691 to bridge the huge chasm that existed between the Church in England as it was and the Church as it should have been at least served to point two valuable lessons, both of which should have been a warning to subsequent generations. The first is that the years 1662 to 1689 had effectively demonstrated the absolute futility and heinousness of coercive and institutional drives for uniformity. The second is that, whatever their secondary differences, believers are to seek the fullest expression of their fundamental unity in Christ, though with the emphatic reminder that such unity and any fellowship based on it must be founded on a firm adherence to the entire Word of God. Co-operation of any other kind is both sinful and bound to be spiritually impotent.

While these attempts at reform were being made in Cheshire, the work of revival in the townships and hamlets of the Peak continued. More and more private householders, whose strong support Bagshawe had gained since the granting of toleration, now applied for licences to register their premises as places of worship. At Ashford, Bagshawe's 'good friend' Henry Hallowes obtained a licence in 1692. John Goodwin of Sheldon made his cottage a sanctuary of Nonconformity; Thomas Swindell registered his barn; and the School House at Mellor, 'in possession of Mr. Cheetham', also received legal sanction.

The Word of God was at this season running a free course. Bagshawe's addresses seemed to be invested with extraordinary power and authority, and both high and low flocked to his chapels. Some out of curiosity, others doubtless more sincere, were anxious to discover for themselves the faith that had sustained the preacher and his congregations under such duress for a quarter of a century. Still others, who had for years been erecting barriers of prejudice between themselves and Bagshawe on account of his Nonconformity, found themselves the object of a constraint more powerful than their prejudices.

A remarkable instance of this kind concerned a local physician, who was reckoned amongst Bagshawe's bitterest opponents. A woman by the name of Stafford, who held Bagshawe's ministry in high regard, was attended by him in her illness. On one particular visit she persuaded him to accompany her to a meeting at which Bagshawe was to preach. During the sermon the preacher suffered a lapse of memory and was obliged to ask his son for the text. Before he could resume, however, the doctor, deeply impressed by what he had already heard, stepped forward and informed the anxious congregation that 'bleeding' would be necessary. Bagshawe was taken to the chapel vestry, where the 'operation' was performed. After warmly thanking the doctor, upon his recovery, Bagshawe resumed his address, which proved to be the means of the doctor's conversion!

With the encouragement of seeing added to the Church such as should be saved, Bagshawe continued his labours with unremitting diligence. The concern he exercised over the young churches of the Peak during these early years of freedom may partly be seen in his practice of visiting each congregation towards the close of the year, to repeat in condensed form the substance of his addresses to them during the previous twelve months! Such regular and systematic instruction probably accounts under God for the immense Scriptural knowledge possessed by his ordinary congregations. Long habits of following him in their Bibles as he elucidated and applied the natural grammatical meaning of Scripture trained them to grasp the arguments of whole chapters and books in a logical way. Nor did Bagshawe leave the instruction of children solely to their parents. Gathering a number of them under one roof, he would catechise and pray with them.

Of the details of Bagshawe's ministry in the early 1690s nothing is known except that he preached, on June 14th, 1693, one of the most memorable sermons of his life. The occasion was a 'fast day', or day of national repentance and thanksgiving authorised by William. Seen in the context of the new-found privileges enjoyed by Nonconformists, the address could not have been more appropriate. Taking as his text Zechariah 1 : 3, 'Turn ye unto Me, saith the Lord of Hosts, and I will turn unto you', Bagshawe reviewed the religious condition of the entire broad sweep of English society, demonstrating the need for repentance in every class.

After commending William III for his 'great design . . . to break tyranny and make way for the establishing of peace and truth', he proceeds to evaluate peers of the realm, ministers of the Gospel, the legal profession, farmers, tradesmen and miners in the light of the eternal law of God. Bagshawe's insistent emphasis on man's perpetual obligation to this law is in fact the most striking characteristic of the sermon. Absolute submission to God alone is his only rule for men and nations. Nothing else, he believed, can preserve a nation from moral decay and give it the enduring stability it requires. If England is to thrive, he seems to say, it will be because God will be pleased to honour her faithfulness to His eternal law. Social, political and economic reforms are all inadequate for the task. Thus, Bagshawe's patriotism is spiritually motivated, springing from a burning desire to honour God.

The other striking feature of this sermon is the tremendous earnestness with which Bagshawe pleads with his own Nonconformist people to guard against complacency. 'Light shines round about us, but does our sight answer our light?' he inquires. The innumerable dangers which a new phase of religious freedom brings must be fought with determination. Pride, self-sufficiency, boasting, back-biting, and other sins all lie waiting at the door, and only humility, prayerfulness, charity, loyalty to the Lord Jesus Christ and active opposition to all sin will succeed against them. Warning his hearers against seeking recrimination for their sufferings in the Great Persecution, Bagshawe warmly commends them to the grace of the Saviour who had upheld them for twenty-five years and who had now granted them liberty. 'Do we rise from our knees with an appetite for the Bread of Life, even the Lord Jesus Christ?' he asks. 'Are we for making mention of His Name, and righteousness, and that only? Is it the great desire of our souls to be found in Christ, not having our own righteousness, but the righteousness which is by faith in Him? We are professors,' he solemnly concludes, 'but are we returners?'

16

Essays on Union to Christ (1693)

The topic of Christian unity, as distinct from ecclesiastical uniformity, having been uppermost in Bagshawe's mind in his connections with the Cheshire Association, he made it the subject of fifteen extended sermons during the early 1690s, stating, however, that their much-requested publication should be deferred until after his death. 'Essays on Union to Christ' is of timeless relevance to all discussions on this subject, since its author lays down the fundamental principles of Christian unity which are applicable in all ages. Here follows a general plan and analysis of the work.

In the first section, Bagshawe deals with the nature of true Christian unity. It is a bond between Christ and His people which originated in the counsel of the Trinity. Christ Himself is the foundation of this bond, and the Holy Spirit, working faith in the believer, is its principal agent. Its subjects are the chosen and redeemed of God.

Section II comprises an exposition of the biblical passages in which this union is presented figuratively, under the similitudes of the lively stone (1 Peter 2 : 4–5); the vine and the branches (John 15 : 5); the head and the body (Ephes. 4 : 15); the husband and wife (2 Cor. 11 : 2).

The third section is an extended treatise on the indwelling work of the Holy Spirit as the 'Fountain (and Spring) of spiritual life and strength', and on the nature of the faith which He produces in believers. As a link with the final section, Bagshawe extracts from Galatians 5 : 24 and 2 Corinthians 5 : 17 two miniature treatises on Mortification of Sin and The New Creature, both of which are models of practical exegesis.

The book closes with a consideration of six privileges enjoyed by those who are united to Christ: they are no longer under condemnation (Rom. 8 : 1); they have an interest in Christ's perfect righteousness (Phil. 3 : 9); they live in hope of glory

(Col. 1 : 27); their souls will immediately be with Christ at death and their bodies sleep in Him (1 Thess. 4 : 14); they shall persevere in grace (1 John 2 : 21); and at Christ's reappearance, they shall judge the world with Him (1 Cor. 6 : 2).

Bagshawe was deeply conscious of the presence within the professing Church of a counterfeit of true unity, namely, external uniformity. Consequently, his purpose throughout the whole treatise is to drive a firm wedge between the genuine thing and its counterfeit. True Christian unity, he asserts, implies a close spiritual relationship between the people of God and Christ their Mediator. Its counterfeit, on the other hand, rests content with attachment to formal and moral observances. 'He that believeth (and not he that is merely joined to the visible church), shall be saved.' Reliance on external performances, even to the extent of being in full communion with a 'reforming congregation', leaves one without Christ.

That true Christian unity is grounded on the accomplished mediatorial work of Christ appears from the fact that it was to unite His people to Himself that Christ 'stooped from heaven to the womb and from thence to the cross'. His whole design in enduring humiliation was to establish the conjugal relationship with His chosen bride, the Church. No other interpretation of His work is adequate to the demands of His Father's justice and His people's need.

That this union with Christ necessitates the indwelling presence of the Holy Spirit arises from the utter inability of God's people by nature to lift a finger towards reconciling themselves to their offended God. The Third Person of the Blessed Trinity must impart life to them, renew and transform them into the image of their heavenly Lord. The genuine believer will unavoidably give proof of his union to Christ by declaring himself a resolute enemy of his former motives, principles and behaviour, and as a new creature in Christ will actively oppose them in the power of his regenerate nature.

By contrast, those in the visible church who remain outside Christ press for 'a sort of conformity', but are guilty of the great sin of nonconformity to Christ. Their counterfeit union bears nothing but counterfeit fruit—grudges, ill-will, and hatred towards the true members of Christ's body. Their worldliness, self-indulgence, and at times sheer devilishness, are permitted to continue unmortified. It is insufficient to be near the Vine: one must be grafted into the Vine.

The next pressing question with which Bagshawe deals is that of how much false friends of Christ may become united to Him. The real reason, he says, why men are separated from Christ is that they are united to sin. However specious 'man's vine' appears, it produces nothing but 'sour, putrid, rotten grapes'. It is under sentence to be cut down and burnt.

Man's union to his sin needs to be broken, and both Law and Gospel are to be instruments employed in the operation. The Spirit of God only convinces men of their sin when the 'gross knife of the Law' is employed to 'cut into' their consciences, reveal to them their inner corruption and moral bankruptcy, and 'cut out' all self-confidence. This 'preparatory work' having been undertaken, the Spirit then takes the 'engrafting instrument of the Gospel' and shows the penitent the spotless righteousness of Christ. Having been brought to renounce all trust in himself and receive by faith this imputed righteousness of Christ, the repentant sinner is truly justified before God. By forsaking every other righteousness but Christ's (and this act of faith is in itself wrought in him by God's Spirit), faith 'fetches Christ into the heart' and so unites its possessor with Him. The language of the redeemed is always: 'Thy favour is freely showed, not to deservers, but to needers; and the unworthy are objects of Thy grace.'

Only one path, therefore, lies open to all who would be united to Christ: 'In the name of Christ, who is all-worthy, go to His Father, for the Spirit,' and plead: 'Lord, Thou hast made believing our duty. O make us able to perform it!'

The third matter which Bagshawe considers is the privileges of the believer. First in point of time is that the terrors of the Law as a Covenant of Works are removed, for there is no condemnation to those who are in Christ Jesus; the criminal is acquitted by the prerogative of mercy exercised by the Crown. Secondly, the believer is richly endowed with 'comforts and pleasures'. 'So exceeding rich is rich grace, that a present worthy (John Howe) worthily wrote—"Unpromised mercies flow on every side".' In times of discouragement, bereavement or oppression, the Saviour imparts consolation; against all opposition, strength; at death, hope; and in the resurrection, glory.

The final question which Bagshawe's treatise throws up concerns the very nature of the Christian Church. Is Nonconformity guilty of the sin of schism? Are its tendencies divisive? To answer this question, Bagshawe asks a further one: 'Are we afraid of schism that is so in the eye of Scripture?' It is to the Word of God as the only authority that he appeals every time. 'We are for all the officers that can prove their institution (and appointment) to be heaven-born, and not for others; and for laws and canons that can abide trying and measuring by the Golden Reed, the Law Canon, or Rule of Holy Writ.' The word of popes, of councils and assemblies, of centuries of tradition, must all give way to the Law of God. Where the Lord Jesus Christ, as sole and undisputed Head of His Church, exercises unquestioned control over men's hearts and lives, there is the true Church. As to the particular form the government of the Church should take, he asserted Presbyterianism as the biblical pattern. Nevertheless, the reader is very conscious that what looms foremost in the author's mind is not the external form but the spiritual life produced by union with Christ. One is left feeling that the ultimate solution to the problems which beset the Church lies not in ecclesiastical machinery and the imposition of outward observances, but in loving obedience to Christ.

17

More Literary Labours (1693-1701)

Sometime in 1693, Bagshawe began to compile a retrospective account of the founding and progress of the North Derbyshire churches during his lifetime. 'De Spiritualibus Pecci, notes (or notices) concerning the work of God, and some of those that have been workers together with God in the Hundred of the High Peak in Derbyshire', occupied his pen intermittently for a further eight years. It was published shortly after its author's death in 1702, largely upon the insistence of John Ashe.

The fact which emerges more conspicuously than any other in Bagshawe's account is that the Peak District experienced a genuine religious awakening during the 17th century. Throughout the long reign of Elizabeth I, with the exception of a few scattered oases of spiritual life, the northern half of the county had been a region of gross spiritual darkness and superstition. Partly, no doubt, owing to its geographical remoteness, the district had been wholly neglected by witness of a distinctly evangelical stamp. But during the Stuart period, in a manner quite inexplicable on natural grounds, the area became subject to unmistakable manifestations of spiritual life and energy. Services were overcrowded, private houses were the scene of much preaching, people in large numbers expressed concern about their souls, morality improved, church discipline was enforced, and the things of eternity became deeply impressed on people's minds. All the signs of a genuine awakening were displayed.

With the exception of the 1630s and early 1640s, when spiritual progress was temporarily hindered by the Laudian persecution, the civil wars and the sloth of unregenerate clergy, the work of the Gospel in the area progressed steadily for a period of sixty or more years, reaching peaks of intensity under the Commonwealth and during the Great Persecution. Bagshawe does not fail to note the convergence on the county in the 1650s of a number of men whose ministries gave considerable stress to reform. Of the churches under persecution, however, he says little. Considering that many of his ejected brethren either left the county or died soon after 1662, Bagshawe's reticence is to be admired, for the heaviest burden of pastoral oversight fell on his own shoulders. Lest he should seem to be praising his own and his living contemporaries' labours, he explicitly refused to take his narrative beyond the 1680s.

A noteworthy feature of the account is the way in which Bagshawe ascribes the origin and progress of the awakening to the sovereign power of God. It is God who chooses, equips and calls into His service the men with whom seasons of spiritual reformation are associated. It is God who grants the increase to their labours. It is God to whom all honour in the salvation of souls is due. The awakening in the High Peak of Derbyshire was a work of pure, free and sovereign grace on the part of God towards His chosen people.

Nevertheless, there exists the closest possible relationship between God's own sovereign work and the faithful employment of divinely appointed means. For this reason, Bagshawe's account is predominantly biographical. He traces the spiritual movement closely, passing under review each person under whose leadership awakening occurred, marking their distinctive qualities and the leading characteristics of their ministry, and assessing their labours in relation to the work of the district considered as a whole.

The narrative commences with one Lady Bowes of Walton, near Chesterfield, who during the second decade of the century established itinerant preachers in the county to remedy the defects of the official clergy. When immorality and failure to preach the Gospel characterised many clergymen of the High Peak, Lady Bowes' 'new Wycliffites' brought light and life to the area. The work begun at her instigation, no doubt at the prompting of the Holy Spirit, was so fruitful that she earned for herself the epithet of 'nursing mother of Nonconformity' in the wild Peak regions. 'That grave divine', John Rowlandson of Bakewell, and his dissenting contemporary, Charles Broxholm, receive special attention among the pioneers. Notable among the remainder are the renowned Isaac Ambrose, 'a star of the first magnitude'; Robert Cryer, a man 'of worth' who laid the foundations for reform at Glossop; 'worthy Mr. Cresswell', whose ministry in Edale made it a 'valley of vision' in his day; the short-lived but Christ-like Anthony Buxton, whom Bagshawe ordained and buried within two years; Thomas Stanley, the 'grave, reverend and tender' Rector of

Eyam: the schoolmaster Samuel Ogden, 'an honour to the Peak';
and Sir John Gell and his wife Catherine, 'no little promoter of
God's work in Derbyshire'. Each is impartially reviewed in the
light of biblical standards of faithfulness and holiness. Anglican
and Dissenter alike are given their place with no suggestion of
partiality. 'Hath not the Lord His witnesses among those of both
(i.e. Anglican and Presbyterian) denominations?' Bagshawe asks,
adding that though he himself had suffered 'much and long' for
his Nonconformity, he could 'heartily bless God for the great good
done by those that conform'. Indeed, a recurring feature of the
narrative is its author's awareness of the unity of believers in
Christ, irrespective of their denomination or social class. His
assessment of Anthony Mellor, curate of Taddington for some
forty years, is illustrative of this point. Though a Conformist, and
though so poor that, like John Bunyan, he was forced to take some
employment in local markets and fairs, he could compel Bagshawe
to cry out: 'O that all Ministers (whether of one Denomination or
another) were his equals in Sobriety and Humility!' In such ways
as this, Bagshawe judges active demonstration of the fruit of the
Spirit rather than denominational or party allegiance to be the
true mark of a genuinely reformed life.

Significantly enough, Bagshawe leaves his readers no narratives
of 'surprising conversions', as does Jonathan Edwards in New
England some forty years later. In fact, his account was not undertaken in the same spirit of scientific inquiry as that of the great
American divine; rather, it constitutes a series of reminiscences,
linked together by the golden thread of sovereign grace which
brought the Derbyshire churches into being. This is the final
impression made upon the mind of a modern reader.

As Bagshawe grew older his spiritual energy was increasingly
renewed. The labours of his last decade of life were quite prodi-
gious. In addition to extensive journeys across the bleak Peakland
moors to his scattered congregations, pastoral visits to private
homes, preaching engagements numbering up to ten per week, he
found time to commit to paper several volumes of 'practical
divinity'. One of these, in four parts, is the quaintly-titled 'Trading
Spiritualised or, Certain Heads, Points, or Positions, on which
Tradesmen (and others) may (O that they would) enlarge in their
Meditations'. Begun in 1694, it was completed two years later and
published by Thomas Parkhurst in London.

Characteristic of Bagshawe's constant endeavours to 'get his eyes down to the level of his hearers' is his homely adaptation of covenant theology to the understandings of his uneducated followers. Following Calvin and the Westminster divines, he asserted that 'Holy Scripture representeth the communion that is between God and man, under the notion or resemblance of commerce or trading'. A fair comparison may be drawn between a trading compact amongst men and spiritual covenanting between God and His people. In both there are distinct parties; terms of trade are laid down and agreed upon, goods and commodities are exchanged.

To acquaint his readers with the unique and exalted nature of spiritual covenanting, Bagshawe commenced with the situation in Eden. A summary of man's pristine estate, in which he stood with 'perfection of grace' written over all his faculties, leads him to admire the goodness of God in 'stooping to' spiritual 'commerce' with Adam. This mutual communion was the glory of innocent man; for this he was made. His fall through disobedience, by which his mind, his affections, his will, his memory and his body were corrupted and vitiated, has rendered such communion no longer possible. The way back to God is closed for ever from man's side. The chief practical lesson, confession of original sin, is then applied: 'If man had kept his first estate, "Hallelujah, Hallelujah" had been much his language', but 'Fallen man hath great cause to fall on his knees (or face) in a way of humiliation'. To close Part I, Bagshawe deals a blow at the Socinians, who claimed death to be the consequence of nature. Death, he replies, is first threatened and then executed solely for sin, and is ascribed throughout the Bible to God's penal justice consequent upon disobedience. As such, death is unnatural.

Part II introduces 'The Sovereign Remedy provided for lost man'. When man cannot retrieve his lost communion with God, when angels cannot help him, God Himself inaugurates a 'blessed transaction' whereby He first gives Himself to His people, then causes them to give themselves to Him. It is out of the richest mercy that God draws up this covenant with Adam and his posterity. Its fountain, therefore, is His free, unmerited, eternal grace and love towards His elect. The agent of the covenant is Jesus Christ, the 'Word which is God, manifest in and made flesh'. The mystery of godliness is then briefly explained: 'God and man met in one Person, that God and man might meet in one (new) covenant

. . . and so in one communion.' So great is the distance between the all-holy and glorious Creator and 'lapsed, ruined man' that the latter dares not think of immediate access to God. The mediatorial work of the Son of God alone can reconcile the two. Under the New Covenant, such a Mediator is necessary, because the transaction is to secure the reconciliation of enemies, whereas the Old Covenant was a 'covenant of friendship'. An enunciation of Christ's threefold office leads to a declaration of His exaltation, and and exhortation to go 'directly (and in a Scripture path) to Christ for supply. This exalted Saviour keeps His heart open to the penitent', but 'His hand will fall and lie heavy on all that are found in wilful impenitency'.

From the work of the Mediator of the New Covenant, Bagshawe turns in Part III to the work of the Holy Spirit, whose indwelling Presence is necessary before 'spiritual commerce' can be resumed between the two parties. Since God is known by His works, Bagshawe considers the Spirit in the various redemptive operations He undertakes. He is first the Spirit of revelation. It is His prerogative to instruct God's covenant people in the 'laws, privileges, and advantages' of the New Covenant. He takes the things of God and reveals them to men; this is spiritual importing. Likewise, He takes the things of men, their minds, their desires, their wills, enlightens and renews them, and carries them to the very courts of heaven through prayer; this is spiritual exporting. At this point, the writer breaks off to express his sense of wonder at the engagement of the all-blessed Tri-une God in the Covenant of Grace. The remainder of this section concentrates on the Spirit's work in regeneration. As natural life is imparted at natural birth, so in regeneration there is an infusion of spiritual life. 'With this new nativity there is a new nature, styled divine, conferred; the regenerate are new creatures.' The subject of regeneration is 'an elect sinner; a sinner, else he needed it not; an elect one, else he obtains it not'. Regeneration is the foundation of all communion with God, for it unites a person to Christ, and therefore to God in Christ. After a further passage on the guiding and leading of the Spirit in the believer's everyday life with God, the section concludes with a few practical exhortations.

In the final part of the work, Bagshawe continues to expound the various operations of the Spirit, and annexes a list of private and public duties. As the Spirit of mortification, He enables believers to pursue a 'vigorous, constant opposition to sin, root and branch'. As the Quickening Spirit, He enlivens the believing mind, conscience, desires, and memory; He establishes the elect in Christ, witnesses in their hearts to Christ, and comforts them in every affliction. Those who are familiar with 'heavenly trade' will exercise faith and hope in, and love to, the Lord, and will engage in secret prayer, spiritual meditation, family prayer, 'edifying conference', hearing God's Word regularly, and the right use of the Lord's Supper. When all these means are faithfully and earnestly employed, the prerogative to render them effectual rests ultimately with the sovereign Lord, and it is to Him that Bagshawe turns in his concluding prayer: 'Alas! Many in effect say to God, we desire not the knowledge of Thy ways. Many (not without knowledge) that were worldly, proud, and sensual, are so still; and beyond a form of godliness too few go, or desire to go. The good Lord pour out of His Holy Spirit, and revive that commerce that savours thereof!'

18

Times of Refreshment (1696-1700)

The early days of 1696 brought to Bagshawe's ministry yet a further season of refreshment from the Lord. The villages of Great Hucklow and Bradwell in particular became the scenes of much blessing. At Hucklow, large numbers were deeply affected when Bagshawe preached on Meekness and on The Blood of the Covenant. Shortly afterwards, when he addressed a packed meeting-house at Bradwell on the topic of 'Diligent Keeping of the Soul', the Word was so borne down upon his hearers that 'tears shot into many eyes' through conviction of negligence and ingratitude. 'It is said and hoped', wrote the preacher undemonstratively, 'that there is some reformation wrought by the Word at Bradwell.'

A sermon on 'Come to the Waters' (Isa. 55 : 1) which he had preached with convicting effects at Bradwell, Bagshawe took to Charlesworth a few days later. But there no such power accompanied the Word. At a 'double lecture' held on March 19th, when the preaching ministry was shared between himself and Robert Moseley, a Cheshire minister, it was Bagshawe for once who spent the largest part of the service listening. 'Mr. Moseley,' he complained ruefully, 'having above three score heads in his solemn sermon, left me little time!'

With the increasing clemency of the weather in April, Bagshawe's preaching engagements grew more frequent. The following fragment gives some idea of the distances he covered on preaching days and of the frequency of his summer engagements:

'1696.   In April, on the second I preached at Macclesfield . . .
On the 7th my labours lay at Bradwell.
On the 8th I preached at Charlesworth.
On the 10th at Chelmorton . . .
On the 14th my work lay at Middleton.
On the 16th at Ashford.'

104

Each Lord's Day, however, saw younger men occupy the pulpits of the churches he had founded, while he returned to the congregations on his own and his brother John's estates, conducting the morning service at Hucklow and evening worship at Malcoff.

A brief glimpse at the church life of these two congregations at this period elicits the fact that the unity of the Spirit in the bond of peace prevailed among them in a remarkable way. The Word of God was powerfully proclaimed, church discipline was enforced, and the sacraments were faithfully administered. The awe-ful significance with which the Lord's Supper in particular was invested was so striking as to lead William Tong, a young minister who attributed his earliest spiritual awakening to one of Bagshawe's communion services, to record an eye-witness account of Bagshawe's practice on these occasions. 'His prayer at the consecration of the elements,' he writes, 'was to an extraordinary degree serious, fervent, and lively: with what a prevalent importunity would he engage the Presence of Christ with His people at His table.' Noting the 'awe-ful reverence' with which Bagshawe handled the elements of bread and wine, 'tho' there were no acts of adoration' to them, Tong was deeply impressed by the way in which he, 'in exhibiting the Seals of the Covenant, would accommodate the special matter and precious promises of that covenant to the particular circumstances of the communicants'. To one recently bereaved, he would say: 'You have lately lost a dear and tender husband, but here is the seal of that covenant whereby your Maker is become your husband, and betroths you to Himself in everlasting loving-kindness.' Similarly, one recently recovered from a severe illness received from him the following encouragement: 'We all looked upon you as a dying person, but God said, "Deliver him from going down to the pit, I have found a Ransome". Here's the Ransome, not of your Life only but of your Soul.' Bagshawe approached the aged in the following tender way: 'Why, you are full of days, bowed down with the infirmities of old age; Christ sends this token to you to assure you that He has not forgotten you, that to your old age He is the same, and to grey hairs He will carry you; be you waiting for His salvation.' In such moving ways did the pastor apply the blessings of the Covenant of Grace to each individual of his flock.

The effects of these communion services on the participants can be imagined. Their faith was strengthened, their love and gratitude to their Saviour was increased, and their peace and joy in the Lord were greatly promoted. Many hard hearts were broken under a sense of ingratitude at grieving such a compassionate Saviour as the Lord Jesus Christ, and the meetings frequently broke up in tears born of the powerful operation of the Spirit. The awareness of the Holy Presence of God sent people away from the meeting house at Malcoff literally trembling and crying out: 'Surely the Lord is in this place! This is none other than the house of God and the gate of heaven!'

Tong's concluding remarks doubtless found an echo in the hearts of many who shared his experience while visiting Bagshawe's churches during such seasons of heavenly blessing: 'How happy a people are these,' he exclaims, 'in having such a pastor, that so thoroughly understands their case, and so naturally cares for their state!'

By midsummer, Bagshawe's preaching activities reached a peak, with engagements almost every day. The 'double lecture' at Charlesworth on June 10th, at which he preached on the Virgin Birth, and the conference at Ashford on the topic of Temperance the day following, were but two of the memorable events which crowded themselves into his diary. A few days later, having toured Edale on a preaching mission, he proceeded to Stockport, where his hearers 'appeared affected' by his sermon on Mortification, 'a spiritual exercise', he commented sadly, 'which is much needed, and too little used'.

For the next three months Bagshawe laboured with unremitting diligence. Whether preaching at Ashford (July 5th), visiting in Glossop (July 29th) or counselling and praying for close friends (August 4th), his energy continued to belie his years. The success accompanying his endeavours refreshed him and encouraged him to persist in the work. It also created new problems. The increasing number of converts in the surrounding villages was beginning to place a severe strain on the existing 'meeting-houses'. The buildings on Thomas Barber's estate at Malcoff, the old barn at Ashford, and the little chapel at Bradwell were no longer adequate to contain the believers, while at Chinley, the homes where he conducted services were full to capacity.

Bradwell was the first to take the initiative. The rugged miners, once uncouth and dissolute gamblers, now pooled their resources towards the erection of an entirely new chapel. 'One fruit of my poor labours ye last year,' commented Bagshawe, 'is ye poor people of Bradwell have prepared a more meet place to meet in.' August 25th, thirty-four years and one day after Bagshawe's ejection, was the date of its official opening. Dissenters from near and far 'flocked in' to rededicate themselves to God and listen to their old pastor expound the great mysteries of the Gospel. 'I preached and prayed, very many heard, and I was assisted,' were his comments on the occasion, while shortly afterwards he noted gratefully that as a consequence of his 'poor endeavours', particularly in insisting on the importance of sanctifying the Lord's Day, 'every Sabbath since then has been less profaned'.

In the closing months of the year, Bagshawe began to seek fresh channels for the Gospel by paying his first recorded evangelising visit to Buxton (September 25th). His reactions to the rapidly-developing spa were significant. 'I went to Buxton,' he records baldly, 'and saw matter for mourning.' Doubtless the immorality which was to gain the spa notoriety during the following century was already in evidence in the 1690s.

Despite the severity of the winter, Bagshawe's love of souls let nothing hinder the diligent discharge of his itinerant duties. 'Serious ministers', he wrote, 'must and do break through the cold and rain when many of their congregation think themselves excused.' On New Year's Day, 1697, his diary records how he and Thomas Barber were lost 'in a close mist' on their way to Castleton and Bradwell to preach, and notes with gratitude their safe arrival 'in due time'.

As his sixty-ninth birthday drew near, however, Bagshawe began to express for the first time his belief that he had little longer to live. When January 17th arrived, therefore, the subject of his address was 'Paul's departure being at hand'. God's time, however, had not yet arrived, and Bagshawe's work continued.

In the ensuing months his life began to follow a pattern similar to that of the previous year. On January 26th he commenced a 'week-night lecture' at Chapel-en-le-Frith; Oliver Heywood and a Mr. Hollingworth visited Ford for prayer and conference on February 3rd; he wrote a tract on Assurance on March 16th; consolidated the work at Middleton in April; and challenged the 'worldliness, vanity, and want of spirituality' at Macclesfield a month later. When August 24th, 'the black day', came round again, he spent it in his customary manner, devoting himself to repentance, fasting, prayer for reformation, and exhorting his family and servants to adhere to the great principles of the Protestant Reformation. During September he was laid aside for a time as a result of a fall from his horse which seriously endangered his life, spending his time in bed writing a treatise on Sins of Omission.

On November 5th, while on the nearby hills celebrations were being held with bonfires and effigies of Guy Fawkes, Bagshawe 'rejoiced moderately' with his family in Ford Hall. A matter so momentous as 'the signal act of the mercy of God in saving the King, the Prince, the Peers, and the Commons from death' called for something other than levity. Accordingly, he reaffirmed his faith in the God of providence, and strengthened their hearts with the hope that He who had so singularly blessed the nation in the past, would not fail to do so in the future. Bagshawe's practice on December 25th likewise betrays a thoroughly biblical attitude to life. Traditional usage he replaced by bringing each member of his congregations before God in prayer, pleading especially that their time might not be consumed in 'indulging the works of the devil which the Lord Jesus Christ came to destroy'. In the days following, he staunchly refused to succumb to the traditions of men, cleaving as of old to the paths into which he had been led half a century before. 'In the concluding days of the year,' he writes, 'I was publicly employed at Charlesworth (having a great congregation), and insisting much on Christ's righteousness as imputed.'

The harsh winter of 1697–98 limited Bagshawe somewhat in the distance, but placed no restrictions on the diligence, of his labours, as the following diary entries testify:

'1698. Jan. 1. I went through the cold to Hucklowe, had many hearers and some help.

2. The Lord's Day, I preached at Malcoff.

4. At Chapel-en-le-Frith.

5. Our solemn thanksgiving at home.

6. At Chinley houses.

7. At Martinside (Kirke family).

10. At Jo(hn) Bagshawe's (his brother).

11. At W. Carrington's (Bugworth Hall).

13. At Marsh Green.

14. At R.M.'s (Robert Middleton).

. . . then I had gone through the round, and been carried comfortably and safely, both on foot and horseback.' This last reference is to his custom of visiting the homes of close friends at the beginning of each new year, to offer special thanksgiving for the mercies of the previous year and to petition God's blessing and protection for the year to come.

For the first six months of the year Bagshawe increasingly confined himself to Ford, reading as voraciously as ever and writing incessantly. By March 20th his growing awareness of his physical decline caused him to bid farewell to the church at Hucklow (notwithstanding which he continued to address them for several years each Lord's Day!), where he commented sadly: 'Friends still fall ill, and alas! I am less able to visit them,' adding on May 28th: 'I drove on at my old pace. O for more progress!' Despite the pleas of his family and advice of his doctor, Bagshawe refused to lay down his charge. 'I do not, I dare not, give up,' he wrote on June 12th, 'O that I went on vigorously!'

As spring blossomed into summer, events in the churches began to take a fresh turn. The work of reconstruction, which had been one of Bagshawe's chief concerns since Toleration, was bearing more fruit. The cumulative effect of the weekly 'double lecture' had produced a spiritually educated generation which was beginning to offer its services in the form of new teachers in the Church. A number of young men had been engaged in itinerant pastoral work as Bagshawe's assistants for some years. Pending acceptance by the local presbytery, they now awaited appointments to particular congregations.

On June 20th, five candidates were summoned to Malcoff for examination. The candidates, John Ashe, William Bagshawe (a relative of the preacher), Joseph Foolowe, ————— Hargreaves, and George Lowe, 'acquitted themselves extraordinarily well', commented William Tong, 'and showed great judgement, seriousness, and humility'.

Having received the approval of the presbytery, the candidates were presented for ordination on the day following. 'I have often thought of the solemnity of that day,' wrote Tong afterwards. 'God was pleased to signalize it greatly . . . the ordainers were graciously assisted and enlarged in their work, especially Mr. Bagshawe, who seemed to excel even himself. . . . In his last prayer, he spoke as one transported with joy, that God had so graciously qualified those young ministers, and admitted them into His service. . . . He observed that there were some present to whom God might now say, "I have taken of your sons and made them Nazarites", and he took particular notice that he himself had the comfort to see one of his near relatives (Ashe), and another of his own name, dedicated to the ministry, and he hoped and prayed that they might do service for God, and the souls of men, when his mouth was stopped; and better service than he had done. . . . These, and many such affectionate things, which in his tender, humble way he then uttered, moved the whole assembly and melted many of them down into a flood of tears.' Thus, with that particular unction which God often bestows upon His faithful servants in their old age, did Bagshawe send to their respective spheres of influence the young men whose growth in grace and in the knowledge of Christ he had carefully watched from their youth.

Now in his seventy-first year, Bagshawe found it increasingly difficult to devote himself to his scattered congregations with the energy of former years. His visits to the more distant churches became less frequent, until by late autumn his sphere of activity was confined to Great Hucklow and Malcoff. Local families remained the objects of his visits, and their children continued to receive catechetical instruction at his hands. The observation he made on his old teacher John Rowlandson was more than ever applicable to himself: 'He remembered the charge given him by the Lord Jesus for the feeding as of His sheep so of His lambs.'

Back in Ford Hall, old friends who paid William and Agnes Bagshawe visits about this time were deeply impressed by the spiritual fragrance of their home. John Ashe, who doubtless spent many hours with them at the Bagshawe table, would not be exaggerating when he described the old Puritan as 'the most affectionate husband, the most careful father, and the kindest master'. His concern for personal holiness overruled every other consideration. He and his wife would gather together his son and 'daughter', with their three children, every morning and evening for prayer and Bible study. Throughout the day, while Samuel was out on the estates, his father would alternate between his study, where he was engaged in a new book, and the drawing-room, where the rest of his family and friends spent their time. The servants, too, were the objects of their concern. Each day Bagshawe and his wife would remind them of their respective duties, spiritual and domestic, and together they 'travailed in birth for them, that Christ might be formed in them'. Little wonder that visitors were reluctant to leave such a sanctuary!

When weather permitted, Bagshawe attended the 'assemblies' of his nearby churches; but for the greater part of the winter and during the early months of 1699 he was engaged in writing thirty-five concise 'treatises of divinity'. Like Thomas Watson's *Body of Divinity*, a work he greatly admired, Bagshawe's own study is based on the Shorter Catechism of the Westminster Assembly. As a popular presentation of the fundamental teachings of the Reformed Faith, it may bear comparison with Dr. J. Gresham Machen's *The Christian View of Man*. Like Machen, Bagshawe, in this collection of essays, displays the peculiar gift of saying the most profound things in the simplest way. A further notable feature of the book is the completeness of the biblical logic which binds together the various strands of thought Bagshawe pursues. With admirable clarity and conciseness, he demonstrates how God's decrees issue in His works of creation and providence, how Adam's fall from righteousness involves the original sin and subsequent misery of all his descendants, how the judicial consequences of sin, by which the way back to God is completely blocked from man's side, must inevitably await God's initiative before fallen man can be reconciled to God, and how Jesus Christ alone must be the sole mediating agent of the Covenant of Grace. Admirable, too, are the sections in which repentance and faith are linked to the respective functions of Law and Gospel.

The reader cannot evade the strong practical emphases of Bagshawe's thesis. Detail in doctrine demands a detailed attention to practice, and here the whole wealth of a lifetime's pastoral experience comes into play. In giving special prominence to the duties consequent upon marriage, upon assuming civic responsibility, and upon entering the Christian ministry, and in spending no less than eleven of the thirty-five sections of the book on such practical issues as prayer, family worship, sin and sins, grace and graces, spiritual privileges and afflictions, Bagshawe shows himself to have remained to the last a guardian of an experimental divinity, a faith which works by love and obedience.

Apart from his customary visits to the homes of local friends and his weekly attendance on the congregations at Hucklow and Malcoff, Bagshawe spent the whole of 1699 and 1700 in literary effort. Uneventful as was his outward life, his 'inner man' reached

I

fresh heights of devotion. His concern for the glory of God and the spiritual well-being of his acquaintances found a new outlet during these closing years of his life in innumerable letters and small manuscript books, which, he said, contained counsel from God which would profit them after his death.

Of the former, only one example is extant, dated January 10th, 1699, and addressed to a Mr. Fletcher, at Attercliffe Presbyterian Academy. After the customary salutations, Bagshawe stresses the greatness of the responsibilities undertaken by faithful preachers of the Gospel. 'When ministers think', he writes, 'of the preciousness of one soul, and their being charged with many, and the account to be given of them, may not every one of them cry out with St. Paul: "Who is sufficient for these things?" ' On the other hand, he adds, the formidableness of the task should not daunt ministerial candidates, for 'there is a sufficiency, (yea, all-sufficiency) in divine grace; and there are, through a Mediator, outflowings of it . . . the God whom ministers serve is infinitely glorious'.

The only extant example of the small manuscript books, dated July 17th, 1700, and intended for the church at Chapel-en-le-Frith, particularly his 'very dear, endeared friends, and children in the Lord', Henry Kirk and Robert Middleton, is incomplete. Quotations from the preface, however, give the gist of Bagshawe's intentions in compiling such booklets:

'Dearly beloved in our best beloved: Feeling (what others see) that mine outward man is decaying; and that divers of the shadows of the evening present themselves to me, I found my heart inclined to pass most of the time which my other employs for God and you would afford me, to compose this piece, as a legacy to be left with you; and though it doth savour of the vessel, of the weakness of him who hath had his eye, and mind, on it for two months; yet I am satisfied that through it God may convey heavenly treasure to those who join *weighing* to the *viewing* of it. . . . O that the substance of this may long live in your hearts! and, if God see it meet, may your prayers prevail that I may for some time longer be a preacher, and prospered therein! The good Lord bless you and yours! and make you and them long blessings! and grant that you may not be losers when you part with too near to worthless and useless old

W. Bagshawe.'

After this affectionate introduction, Bagshawe proceeds to enumerate what he calls 'Twelve principles of the oracles of God and doctrine of Christ, being prime dictates of the Holy Spirit'. They are worth quoting in full as a compact summary of his doctrinal views.

'Heb. xi. 6	The first point (or article) of faith to which right reason assenteth is—That God is.
Gen. i. 26–28 and ii. 17	A second is—When God made man at first, or the first man, He made him in His image, intelligent, righteous, holy; and made a holy covenant with him, usually called the covenant of Works, or of Nature. Obedience personal, perfect, and perpetual, which he was fitted for, was required on man's part; and life, with happiness, was thereupon put into God's promise.
Rom. v. 12	A third is—The first man kept not his first estate, but fell by sin, breaking at once the law and covenant of God; and all that derive from him, fell with him. By committing high treason, his blood was attainted. As man, so mankind was ruined.
Rom. vi. 23	The fourth is—Fallen man lieth in the mouth of death, and wrath.
2 Sam. xxiii. 5	The fifth is—According to the agreement among (and between) the three Persons in the all-blessed and undivided Godhead from eternity, a covenant of grace and life is made, in time.
Heb. xii. 23, 24 1 Tim. ii. 5 Col. i. 19, 20 Heb. i. 1–3	The sixth is—The Redeemer (and Recoverer) of man, the Mediator of the new covenant, is the Lord Jesus Christ; the Son of God; who became man, and in man's nature the greatest sufferer and only satisfier of Divine justice, and meriter of Divine mercy on man's behalf.

John v. 39	The seventh is—In the Scriptures of truth, and writings from heaven, there is a fair edition of the covenant of grace.
John vi. 35 and vii. 37 Rev. xxii. 17	The eighth is—To all that read (and hear) the Gospel: grace in (and with) Christ is tendered and offered.
1 John v. 12 John i. 12	The ninth is—Sincere embracers (and receivers) of Christ by faith have Him, and life with Him.
	The tenth is,—That any are such, is owing, and to be ascribed to the special work and call of the Holy Spirit.
	The eleventh is—The effectually called have a great change of their state and frame in justification and sanctification.
Rev. iii. 18–20	The twelfth is—Whilst others through refusal (or want) of grace perish, the justified and sanctified enjoy precious privileges here, and shall enjoy eternal life hereafter.'

The only other information we possess of Bagshawe's activities during 1700 concerns a small *System of Divinity*, still in manuscript form. This 'fresh essay towards an exact sum and system or Body of Divinity' was 'begun with some dependence on Divine assistance on ye eighth day of 1700 at three in ye afternoon'. Duplicating as it does so much of the material in the thirty-five 'treatises,' its chief claim to remembrance rests in the expression it gives to its author's intense love for his God and Saviour. Mind and heart are at one, and both find their rest in the all-blessed Creator and Redeemer.

19

Last Days and Death (1701-02)

By the summer of 1701, Bagshawe's physical weakness was taking a greater toll of his ministerial duties. The extensive preaching journeys of his former years were undertaken by his young assistant, John Ashe, Bagshawe confining himself to the meeting-house at nearby Malcoff. As late autumn hardened into winter, he felt unable to visit even Malcoff, and resorted to preaching in his own home. There at Ford Hall, with the wisdom and unction of a patriarch, he received sufficient strength to expound the Scriptures each week to gatherings of his family and close friends.

The comfortable state of mind in which Bagshawe spent these declining months is testified by his will, which was drawn up on October 15th. This remarkable document begins in the following way: 'I, William Bagshawe . . . commit my precious and immortal spirit into the hand of the all-blessed and undivided Trinity, my powerful, and faithful Creator, Redeemer, Sanctifier, and Comforter; bewailing the sin of my heart and life; in particular my many and manifold failures former and fresher, as to the discharge of the weighty ministerial charge by me undertaken; fleeing to and relying on, the free grace of God the Father, held forth in and through the merit and mediation of the Lord Jesus Christ, who in my nature hath fulfilled all righteousness, satisfied infinite justice, and procured forfeited mercy for believing penitents waiting in heaven's way for pardon and salvation; professing myself a member of the truly called Catholic and Universal Church of Christ, and an honourer of that famous part thereof that is in Old and New England, and elsewhere; holding inward communion with all the faithful; and outward with all the owners of the truth so far as I can without sin; and longing for a more full and Scriptural Reformation. And as I hope for the glorifying of my soul immediately after its leaving my body, so I believe that at the last and great day, my body (the decent interring whereof I desire), though it should not be admitted into a place styled consecrated, shall by

115

Divine power and grace be raised, and reunited to my soul, that I may be ever with the Lord.'

On November 11th his beloved wife died. Through half a century she had borne with inimitable patience the trials laid on her as a partner and co-worker of one of the most heroic Nonconformists of the century. A woman of decidedly Puritan sentiments and firm Christian character, Agnes Bagshawe had graced her husband's home with meekness and good works. Under her care and supervision, Ford Hall had been a place of refuge for persecuted Dissenters, a hospitable training ground for ministerial candidates, and a prayer and conference centre for the leading Nonconformist ministers of the Peak. She had 'looked well', not merely to the ways of her own household, but also to the 'household of God'.

Though in failing health, William Bagshawe survived the winter and appeared to make some recovery by March. But the end of his earthly course was near. On receiving news of the death of 'his dear sovereign', William III, he prepared what proved to be his last sermon, expounding Romans 8 : 31, 'What shall we then say to these things? If God be for us, who can be against us?' On March 22nd he is reported to have preached with such life and vigour that a stranger would have thought him in perfect health. Eye-witnesses caught on to the prophetic remark, made towards the close of his address, that: 'Who knows, but God may in this age make use of a Queen of England to break the power of France, as in a former age He made use of one to break that of Spain.' When he had finished, however, 'he was sensible that his preaching work was over, and judged it would be tempting God to make another essay'.

His weakness increased daily until the following Lord's Day, when he was unable to leave his bed. On being invited to speak a few words to his assembled family, he replied: 'My silence is a sermon.' Realising the hour of his death drew nearer, friends such as the Kirkes of Martinside and the Carringtons of Bugworth Hall called to pay their last respects during the closing days of March, but he was unable to speak to them for more than a few minutes. He disclosed to one friend, however, that the doctrine of the imputed righteousness of Christ was his constant support during his 'languishing state', and that he was 'well-satisfied' with his Nonconformity, blessing God 'who had kept him from acting against his conscience in that affair'. His hopes of heaven, noted Ashe, though lacking those 'transporting ecstasies' that some experience, were 'solid and well-grounded'.

A young minister who received permission to pray with him on one occasion at this time observed that Bagshawe 'joined heartily in every petition', thanked him for his kindness, and praised the Lord for helping him 'to such apt expressions'. He then remarked, on wondering why people were so opposed to extempore prayer: 'There is not a prayer in all their book (of Common Prayer) would have suited my present circumstances so well as this has done.'

On Wednesday, April 1st, Bagshawe's debility increased, yet his mind continued unclouded and his body free from pain. By nightfall, he asked for a hymn. Having first attempted to sing every line with those at his bedside, he added 'Amen', and then, writes Ashe, 'without the least groan or struggle, surrendered his pious soul into the hands of his Redeemer, and went to his everlasting rest'.

Attended by large numbers from every part of the Peak District, William Bagshawe's earthly remains were interred beneath the chancel of Chapel-en-le-Frith parish church on April 5th. John Ashe's subsequent sermon (on Hebrews 13 : 7) and tribute deeply impressed the minds of his hearers with a sense of the great loss they had sustained by the death of their beloved pastor, and forcefully reminded them of the tremendous debt they owed God for granting them such a man as Bagshawe had been. 'We have seen the beauty of practical godliness exemplified in him,' said Ashe, 'and the several graces of the Divine Spirit exercised to such a degree as very few arrive at.' But now, 'we no longer enjoy his presence, nor shall we any more receive the Divine Law at his lips. That mouth which so often and pathetically treated of Divine things in your hearing, is locked up in silence till the Resurrection of the just.'

Appendix I

COMMEMORATION PLAQUE
AT CHAPEL-EN-LE-FRITH

The following entry in the parish register of Chapel-en-le-Frith relates to Bagshawe's burial:

'1702. April. Mr. William Bagshawe of the Fford, Nonconformist Minister, was buried in the chancell.' In a later hand is added: 'Styled "the Apostle of the Peake".'

Above the chancel is a plaque commemorating his life and work in the following terms:

'To make known and to keep in men's memories the worthy deeds of a former inhabitant of this parish, William Bagshawe, of Ford Hall, named the Apostle of the Peak. This inscribed stone is erected in compliance with the will of his grandson hereafter mentioned. He was the eldest son of William Bagshawe of Abney, Litton, Hucklow and Ford, was born at Litton, Jan. 17, 1628, educated at Corpus Christi College, Cambridge, ordained a minister of the Church of England when that Church was Presbyterian: exercised his office at Wormhill, at Sheffield, and in the neighbouring parish of Glossop, of which he was for 11 years the vicar. After the restoration of episcopacy, being unable to comply with the terms of the celebrated act of 1662 he resigned his ecclesiastical preferment and retired to Ford Hall, his patrimonial inheritance. But though he ceased to be a minister of the established church, he did not allow himself to be divested of his character of a minister of the Word of God. Like the Apostles Peter and John (Acts 5 : 42) he ceased not to teach and to preach both at his own house and from house to house. Nor did he labour in vain. Throughout these wild regions a spiritual awakening such as had never before been witnessed followed his exhortations, and multitudes were led to accept from his lips the offer of eternal life. Free grace through a crucified Redeemer was the theme which produced so mighty a result, for although Mr. Bagshawe was very careful to press moral duties, yet he was far more solicitous to unfold the mystery of the Gospel and to proclaim the unsearchable riches of Christ, being fully satisfied that unless men be washed in his blood, clothed with his righteousness, and animated by his Spirit, their highest attainments and most splendid performances will leave them short of heaven.

'For forty years this parish was the centre of his evangelistic efforts, which embraced the whole of North Derbyshire. Towards the close of his life the infirmities of age obliged him gradually to transfer to others the oversight of the numerous congregations which he had gathered and on the 1st. of April, 1702, he fell asleep in Jesus, resting all his hopes on that imputed righteousness of which he had so often preached. His remains are interred in the chancel of this church.'

Appendix 11

BAGSHAWE'S LITERARY WORKS

1653   *Waters for a Thirsty Soul*, or *The Water of Life* (Sermons on Revelation 21 : 6) [lost]

1653   *Of Christ's Purchase*, to which is prefixed his *Confession of Faith* [lost]

?   *Rules for our daily walk, for sanctifying the Sabbath, with an help for communicants* [lost]

1658   *Brief Directions for the Improvement of Infant Baptism* [lost]

1671   *Principiis Obsta*, comprising 'The Ready Way to Prevent Sin' and 'A Bridle for the Tongue', short treatises on Proverbs 30 : 32 and Matthew 12 : 36

1674   *The Riches of Grace*, Part I

1674   *The Privilege of Passive Obedience*, or *Sheet for Sufferers*

1674   *Matters for Mourning*, or *52 Posing Proposals in order to the helping of Heart-humiliation*

1675   *The Miner's Monitor*, or *A Motion to those Whose labour lies in and about the Lead and other mines* [lost]

1681   *Expository Notes on the Song of Solomon* [unpublished]

1683   *Miscellaneous Treatises* [unpublished]

?   *Treatise on the Holy Spirit* [unpublished]

?   *The Sweetest Constraint*, 9 sermons on 2 Corinthians 5 : 14 [unpublished]

?   *Sermon Notes* (2 volumes) [unpublished]

1685   *The Riches of Grace*, Parts II and III

?   *The Sinner in Sorrow and the Humble Sinner's Modest Request* [lost]

1686–87   cir. *Treatise on Popery* [unpublished]

1693–1701   *De Spiritualibus Pecci*

1694   *Trading Spiritualised*, Part I

1695   *Trading Spiritualised*, Part II

1696   *Trading Spiritualised*, Parts III and IV

1696–97–98   Diary (extant only for 3 years) [unpublished]

1698   *35 Treatises on Divinity* [unpublished]

1700   *System of Divinity* [unpublished]

1703 (posth.)   *Essays on Union to Christ*

TODAY'S GOSPEL—AUTHENTIC OR SYNTHETIC?

Walter J. Chantry

This is an arousing new book by the pastor of Grace Baptist Church, Carlisle, Pennsylvania in which he expounds from Christ's dealing with the Rich Young Ruler the essential elements in Gospel preaching. A close examination of the Scripture evidence leads to this conclusion:

'Differences between much of today's preaching and that of Jesus are not petty; they are enormous. The chief errors are not in emphasis or approach but in the heart of the Gospel message. Were there a deficiency in one of the areas mentioned in these pages, it would be serious. But to ignore all – the attributes of God, the holy law of God, repentance, a call to bow to the enthroned Christ – and to pervert the doctrine of assurance, is the most vital mistake.

'Incredulity may grip you. Can so many evangelicals be so wrong? . . . All are not in error, but great hosts are. All have not perverted the Gospel to the same degree, but many are terribly far from the truth. All those who "make decisions" are not deceived, but great numbers are. Above all, few *care* to recover the Gospel message . . .'

This powerfully written book has a message which goes to the heart of the contemporary problem in a way that conferences and commissions on Evangelism have failed to do. Its positive expository approach is particularly valuable.

96 pages, paperback, 4s

GENEVA SERIES OF COMMENTARIES

*Genesis *John Calvin*	1088 *pp*, 35*s*
Leviticus *Andrew Bonar*	544 *pp*, 25*s*
Psalms *David Dickson*	1056 *pp*, 25*s*
*Proverbs *Charles Bridges*	656 *pp*, 30*s*
*Daniel *John Calvin*	816 *pp*, 30*s*
Jonah *Hugh Martin*	372 *pp*, 15*s*
Zechariah *T. V. Moore*	250 *pp*, 15*s*
Haggai and Malachi *T. V. Moore*	180 *pp*, 10*s* 6*d*
*John *William Hendriksen*	768 *pp*, 30*s*
Acts *J. A. Alexander*	984 *pp*, 25*s*
Romans *Robert Haldane*	660 *pp*, 21*s*
*I Corinthians *Charles Hodge*	400 *pp*, 15*s*
*II Corinthians *Charles Hodge*	320 *pp*, 12*s* 6*d*
*Galatians *William Hendriksen*	272 *pp*, 21*s*
*Ephesians *Charles Hodge*	418 *pp*, 15*s*
*I & II Timothy and Titus *William Hendriksen*	408 *pp*, 21*s*
James *Thomas Manton*	482 *pp*, 21*s*

*Not for sale in the U.S.A. or Canada.

SOME PAPERBACK TITLES

An Alarm to the Unconverted
    Joseph Alleine   160 *pp*, 4s 6d

The Best Books *W. J. Grier*   176 *pp*, 4s 6d

The Bible Tells Us So *R. B. Kuiper*   144 *pp*, 5s

*The Christian View of Man
    J. Gresham Machen   240 *pp*, 5s

Fair Sunshine *Jock Purves*   208 *pp*, 5s

Five Christian Leaders *J. C. Ryle*   192 *pp*, 4s 6d

Five English Reformers *J. C. Ryle*   160 *pp*, 3s 6d

For a Testimony [*illustrated*] *Bruce F. Hunt*   160 *pp*, 5s

*God-Centred Evangelism *R. B. Kuiper*   240 *pp*, 6s

The Gospel in Exodus *Henry Law*   176 *pp*, 5s

John Bunyan *Frank Mott Harrison*   232 *pp*, 5s

Letters of John Newton   192 *pp*, 4s 6d

The Mystery of Providence *John Flavel*   224 *pp*, 4s 6d

Prayer *John Bunyan*   176 *pp*, 4s 6d

The Rare Jewel of Christian Contentment
    Jeremiah Burroughs   240 *pp*, 4s 6d

Reformation Today *Klaas Runia*   160 *pp*, 5s

*Roman Catholicism *Loraine Boettner*   560 *pp*, 8s 6d

Romans *Geoffrey Wilson*   256 *pp*, 6s

*A Summary of Christian Doctrine *Louis Berkhof* 192*pp*, 3s 6d

SOME OTHER TITLES

An All-Round Ministry *C. H. Spurgeon*	418 *pp*, 15*s*
A Body of Divinity *Thomas Watson*	328 *pp*, 15*s*
Charity and Its Fruits *Jonathan Edwards*	382 *pp*, 21*s*
The Christian Ministry *Charles Bridges*	408 *pp*, 25*s*
The Christian in Complete Armour *William Gurnall*	1200 *pp*, 35*s*
George Whitefield's Journals [*illustrated*]	596 *pp*, 25*s*
The Interpretation of Prophecy *Patrick Fairbairn*	546 *pp*, 25*s*
John G. Paton: Missionary to the New Hebrides	528 *pp*, 21*s*
The Log College *Archibald Alexander*	256 *pp*, 21*s*
A Narrative of Surprising Conversions *Jonathan Edwards*	256 *pp*, 15*s*
The Office and Work of the Holy Spirit *James Buchanan*	296 *pp*, 21*s*
Robert Murray M'Cheyne: Memoir and Remains *Andrew A. Bonar*	660 *pp*, 25*s*
Simon Peter *Hugh Martin*	160 *pp*, 12*s* 6*d*
Spurgeon: The Early Years [*illustrated*]	570 *pp*, 25*s*
*Systematic Theology *Louis Berkhof*	780 *pp*, 35*s*
The Ten Commandments *Thomas Watson*	240 *pp*, 15*s*
The Works of John Flavel: 6 vols	£6 6*s the set*
The Works of John Owen: 16 vols	25*s each*